YOU ARE MY SISTER

written by

ANFRA

Published and Distributed by:
F.I.G. Publishing
2760 Cracklerose
Memphis, TN 38127

Second Printing August 1999

ISBN 0-9673491-0-9
Library of Congress Catalog Card Number: 99-96350

Cover designed by 16 year old Shawn Williams

Printed in the United States by:
Morris Publishing • 3212 East Highway 30 • Kearney, NE 68847

F.I.G. PUBLISHING

"Write the vision"

ABOUT THE AUTHOR

Anfra Boyd is an author, poet and inspirational speaker. She started the on-line column *You Are My Sister* on her former job in Corporate America as a means to inspire her co-workers. Since then, the column is being read by women around the world.

She's also a novelist, with two novels soon to be published and conducts workshops and speaks to women around the world. She also mentors teenagers with her inspiration and uses her home as a safe haven where teenagers come to have fun, learn, and have someone to talk to.

Anfra is also member of the Board of Directors for the Black Writers Conference and Southern Film Festival in Memphis, TN. Her messages and poetry are featured on web sites all across the Internet, and she's had articles published with several women's magazines and newsletters. She's also the founder of the on-line book club YAMS, that promotes literary entrepreneurs and the self-published community.

To book a speaking engagement or workshop contact:

MSANN2U@aol.com
www.anfra.com
901-353-2665

DEDICATIONS

My Grandmothers:

Mrs. Daisy Pearl Jones
Mrs. Rebecca Boyd
&
Ms. LaBertha Miller
Mrs. Mildred Hunt
Mrs. Mae Parker
Mrs. Freddie Harvey

In loving memory of the women who touched my life and left a lasting impression. Your spirits will be with me always.

TO THE LATE:

Rev. R. V. Kinnard

Thank you for setting me on my spiritual path. You'll always be in my heart.

THANKS -GIVING

First of all I would like to thank God for anointing my life with wisdom and inspiration. Thank you, Father!!!

My parents, Leroy and Beatrice Boyd, for unconditional love and support throughout my life.

My son Cameron, the love of my life, thanks for being my number one fan. My nieces and nephews, Rebecca, Adrienne, Michael, Tina and Reba for keeping me in-line and listening to my words of wisdom. My sister Pamela for making copies of the column and passing them out on her job.

To my Aunt Maggie Wilson, your words of wisdom started me on my spiritual journey.

To Angela Robinson for your support. You've been at every speaking engagement and poetry slam, constantly cheering me on. Thank you.

To Mr. Marvin Dejean, author of the on-line column *The Prime Directive* for your unconditional love and support. Your friendship came at a time when I needed it the most.

To Maxine Thompson, author of *No Pockets In A Shroud*, thanks for being my friend and sharing your wonderful talent with me.

To my good friend Michelle Shelton, for all of your support and help during the years.

To my aunt, Dorothy Bowman, for giving me a beautiful name.

To Lawrence Wayne, founder of the Black Writers Conference in Memphis, thanks for your encouragement and support.

To Kim Lewis at Destination Radio in Springfield Mass, thanks for the invitation to the SisterFriends Weekend, and all of your support. YOU ARE MY SISTER.

To Kem Warnette at Sidewalk University, thank you for giving me my first opportunity to get published in *GRACE* magazine. You believed in me when no one else thought I could write.

And last but not least, thanks to all the Sisters around the world who read the on-line column and forwarded the e-mail to all of their family and friends. Because of you, the on-line column is now a book. Thank you. God Bless and remember You Are My Sister!

AUTOGRAPH PAGE

TO: _Nicole Davis_

YOU ARE MY SISTER

Dedicated to promoting sisterhood and spiritual growth.
Its purpose is to encourage, enlighten and empower

SISTERS

God Bless and remember
You are my Sister

Onifre
9/19/99

INTRODUCTION

The messages contained in this book are not my own and were totally inspired by God. I was just the secretary taking dictation for the **CEO of Life**. We are living in a time when women are spiritually and emotionally bankrupt. Modern women are searching for peace, happiness and love; You Are My Sister serves as a road map.

This book promotes sisterhood and spiritual growth. Its purpose is to encourage, enlighten and empower sisters. The inspirational messages within these pages are thought provoking. As they are based on life's lessons of love, spirituality and empowerment. The reader will be challenged to move to a higher level of self-love, self-respect and self-worth.

Upon finishing this book, I hope that you will be inspired and moved to make a change in your life, as well as come to the understanding that we're all connected and have a purpose in God's universe.

God bless and remember You Are My Sister.

Anfra

A TRIBUTE TO AFRICAN-AMERICAN AUTHORS

It is in the **HEART OF A WOMAN** to believe that we should have a man in our lives. It doesn't matter how we look, kinky hair, straight hair or **GOOD HAIR**, we believe there's a man out there for us, one who's been taught by his **MAMA** to treat us with respect and dignity. In our search for **A DO RIGHT MAN,** we've done some **SCANDALOUS** things with our bodies and our minds. We've been licked and sticked and sucked until now the men out there are **NEVER SATISFIED.** They want us to treat them like kings, when actually they aren't worthy. They think their loving is **SO GOOD**, and we are so **CAUGHT UP IN THE RAPTURE** with them that we forget **LI'L MAMA'S RULES.** When one relationship fails, we're on the look out for **ONE BETTER** than the last one, **KNOWING** that the next relationship will be the right one.

Mr. Right, or Mr. Right Now, is out to prove that he can win us over with his good looks and conversation. Once we let him into our lives he starts to playing **DISAPPEARING ACTS** on us. His **INVISIBLE LIFE** starts to call, and he has to answer, leaving us questioning our judgment of men. We start to ask ourselves why can't I find someone who will accept me **JUST AS I AM? BEHIND CLOSED DOORS** this man was all that I wanted. Good sex, attentive, fun, you know a roughneck brother that's what we like.

We've all graduated from the school of **HARD KNOCKS** and should know better by now. All of us have experienced **SOME LOVE, SOME PAIN, SOMETIME**, but we have to accept and believe **AND THIS TOO SHALL PASS.** In our **SEARCH FOR SATISFACTION**, we've made a lot of mistakes and find it hard **TRYIN' TO SLEEP IN THE BED YOU MADE.** We promise ourselves that we **AIN'T GONNA BE THE SAME FOOL TWICE**, instead we're the same fool over and over, and over again. We should try practicing **ACTS OF FAITH** to keep us strong and holding on.

Women are **LAUGHING IN THE DARK**, while **MEN CRY IN THE DARK**, when they think the **DEVIL'S GONNA GET HIM**, when actually he was chasing **A DEVIL IN A BLUE DRESS. IF THIS WORLD WERE MINE**, I would make sure that every woman in this world had a good man, but since it's not, I'm glad that we all are *not* **WAITING TO EXHALE.**

So, from one **SISTER, SISTER**, we've got to start acting more like **BROTHERS & SISTERS**, instead of **SISTERS & LOVERS** or **FRIENDS & LOVERS** so that we can all be happy and respect each other like family, and put away all of our **UGLY WAYS.**

SISTERHOOD CREED

I promise to be true to myself

to let my conscious and inner spirit be the guide to my
      moral values

to honor and respect God, myself and others at all times

to think, speak and live positively and restrain from
      all negative forces

to live in peace, happiness, joy and love each day

to live in truth

to spend quality time with myself in order to improve
      on my quality of life

to end all bad relationships and start new ones with
      honesty and trust

to end criticism, worry and fear in my life

to learn from my past mistakes and not repeat them

to give of my time freely to help others

to uplift and encourage my sisters

to bring unity to my family and community

to set an example for future generations

to appreciate the beauty of the universe and all
      living creatures

to constantly strive for higher education and spirituality

to begin and end each day with Love!!

YOU ARE MY SISTER

14

SISTERS

Are we really sisters? What is it that bonds us together? Is it family, friendship, neighbors, church, community or what? Well, I think the answer is the spirit. We are sisters because we share the same Father in heaven, the same spiritual blood, and that means that we should treat each other with respect and dignity. We should celebrate our differences and share our faith and love. We should encourage each other and humble ourselves to the truth. We should all do some soul searching first and find out what's important in life. Find out where our hearts are and what do we treasure most in life. Do we treasure the wrong things? money, men, clothes, cars, jobs and our children. Do we have inner peace and joy? Can we surrender our bodies totally to our Father in heaven?

Soul searching requires time alone without interruptions from the TV, radio, children, etc. Spend some time alone with yourself and find out if you even like yourself. What you'll find out will amaze you. A lot of us don't even know ourselves, yet we expect everyone else to. Ask yourself some questions: Am I being a sister? What areas of improvement do I need? Am I knowingly dating the wrong man? Am I dating my sister's husband? Am I violating my sister's life in any way? Am I being violated by one of my sisters? You and only you can answer these questions honestly. Spend sometime alone my sisters and find the real you. The revelation you'll find will change your life completely. Think about it, sisters!!

WHO ARE YOU?

"When I discover who I am ... I'll be free"
- Ralph Ellison "Invisible Man"

Who are you? Can most of us answer that question with conviction and confidence? Do you really know who you are? A child of God is the answer that most of us would reply. But, besides being a child of God, who are you? A wife, mother, sister, friend, and employee. What's your purpose in life?

When I read this quote in an e-mail, the words had a profound affect on my spirit, because the words are so true, and describe exactly how I feel since I've discovered who I am. Now that I know who I am, I'm free.

When you discover who you are, you've found your purpose in this journey of life. And, until you find your purpose and live your purpose, you're in bondage, enslaved to others around you: your environment, family and friends. Your life is not your own and you live each day trying to please others, and constantly need acceptance and approval for decisions about your own life. You look for others to love you, make you happy and to have the answers for your dilemmas in life.

Discovering who I am, was a life changing and powerful experience for me. I discovered that no one on this earth has power or authority in my life. I am responsible for my own soul, and in control of my own destiny. I can go to God for everything that I need and want, and He gives me the answers, and supplies all of my needs. I no longer seek approval from others, or need their opinion for what my purpose is in life.

When you discover who you are, your spirit will be free. You'll be free of tradition, religion, other's expectations, rules and regulations. You'll be free to live the life God intended for you. Free to rise above the expectations of your family and friends. Your life will have harmony and peace and your purpose will be in sync with your spirit. Your creativity will awaken, and you'll discover how spiritual life really is. Who are you? Think about it, sisters!!!

THE NEW MILLENNIUM

We're less than a year away from the 21st century, — the new millennium. During the 20th century, African-American women have overcome many hardships and won many triumphs. We owe many of our privileges we have today to numerous women throughout the last century,- Rosa Parks, Gwendolyn Brooks, Alice Walker, Madam C. J. Walker, Shirley Chism, Maya Angeleou, Debbie Allen, Oprah Winfrey, Iyanla Vanzant and Susan Taylor, to name just a few. We've gone from picking cotton in the hot fields, being nannies and caretakers, to owning our own companies and TV shows. In the last twenty years of this century there's been a revolution happening for the black woman. We're writing our own legacy for the next generation, from politics, fashion, technology, entertainment, to space, we are there.

Are we prepared for the next century, the new millennium? What can we expect and what do we want? Like our heroines of yesterday and today, we too have a purpose in life, a calling to fulfill. When Rosa sat down on that bus in Alabama over 30 years ago, she probably didn't realize at that moment her calling in life was happening. She was just tired and didn't want to get up and give her seat to someone white. The rest is history, her calling to be the Mother of the Civil Rights Movement. Where will you be when you answer your calling? You see, we all have a calling in life that simply means a purpose, a reason for living

Everything in life has a purpose, the sun, moon, earth, the rain, the grass, the animals and YOU.

Your purpose in life, whether it's writing, mentoring, preaching, teaching, or whatever, is to bring fulfillment to God's creation. Giving, sharing, educating, inspiring, caring, these are just some of the adjectives that describe life's purpose, "a calling." Having purpose and being on purpose means giving of yourself to help others in some way.

As sisters let's get prepared for the new millennium. We can start by evaluating our lives and the ways that we're living. We can become world visionaries and spend our money and our time doing our life's work, God's work. Let's leave behind our bad relationships and experiences. Leave behind hatred, jealousy, envy, prejudice and guilt. Let's leave behind all the negative spirits in the 20th century and focus on being a positive spirit in the 21st. Finding your purpose in life is not that difficult, and most of us already know what it is, but we're hesitant about doing it. Hesitant because we think others won't accept us or like us for speaking out and standing up, or we think we don't have enough time.

Let's enter the new millennium with purpose. When you have purpose in your life, your life has meaning and fulfillment. You'll feel compelled to do more each day to make the world a better place. With purpose you won't have time to focus on the things in life that you don't have, and you'll use what you have to help yourself and others. Think about it, sisters!!!

19

VISION OF LIFE

What is your vision of life? Do you have a Polaroid, 110 or 35mm view of life? Are you seeing life through a Polaroid shot, where you only see yourself and the few people in your life, your family, friends, job, relationship. Like a Polaroid shot, is everything in your view instant, love, sex, gratification, and justice? Do you want everything right now this instant, and once you have it or do it, it's over and you're not satisfied with the outcome, the results, the picture?

Maybe you have a 110 view of life, where you can add a few more people in your view and wait on the results. You're willing to wait for the outcome and get a chance to take more than one shot. Are you willing to wait a little longer for love, sex, gratification and justice? Then once you get the results back you realize that your view was off and the picture didn't focus in on the background or you couldn't see the small details that were so important and it's too late now to take another picture.

Maybe you have a 35mm view of life and you're willing to focus in on the more important things in life, and not just yourself. Maybe you can focus in on the injustices of the world, or better yet, you can focus on the beauty of it. With a 35mm view you can zoom in on the smallest things in your view, like the butterflies, flowers, children laughing and playing. In your 33mm view you can include the sunshine or the beauty of a cloudy day, even the rain. With a 35mm view you're willing to wait even longer for love, sex, gratification and justice because you want to get all the important details to make sure the picture is clear and precise.

Hopefully you have a 35mm view of life and you're focused and able to wait for the outcome and the results of the pictures you took. More importantly, make sure that whatever view you have, whether it's Polaroid, 110 or 35mm you keep your shutters open. Think about it, sisters!!!!

"LISTENING COMES BEFORE UNDERSTANDING, UNDERSTANDING COMES BEFORE WISDOM"

How many times have you been sitting at a red light and when the light changes to green "something" tells you to sit there a minute before pulling off? While you're sitting there, a car coming in the other direction runs the red light and you sit there for a moment horrified and find yourself saying, " Oh, thank God I waited."

Have you ever been awakened by "something" suddenly and getting up to find something wrong in your home, like the door left unlocked or your child or loved one crying or hurting? Maybe "something" told you to call a friend or relative that you haven't talked to in a long time and you find out that they were just thinking about you too.

What is that "something" that alerts us to danger, and hurt or keeps us from acting too fast or moves us quickly? What is that inner voice that tells us right from wrong, although most of us haven't learned to listen to it at all times? Only when something happens do we think in retrospect ,"something told me to...." We'll find ourselves saying, "I should of followed my first mind."

That "something" is the "Spirit," the Voice of God, something that we all have and has been with us from the moment of conception. Our spirit is born before we enter into the world from our mother's womb. Learning to listen to your spirit can help you make wise decisions in life. When the Spirit speaks to you, it gives you the right answers for your life's work. The Spirit not only alerts you to danger and hurt or when something is wrong; it also speaks to you on a daily basis, 24-7. At all times the Spirit is with you guiding you to safety or telling you what you should or should not do each day. Our teachings at home, school and society in general teach us to look outwardly for the things in life that we need or want, when actually the answers to everything we need and want are on the inside, where God's indwelling Spirit is.

How do we learn to listen to our Spirit? One of the ways, and the most effective, is "prayer" on a daily basis. Not just when you're in a bad situation or want something (husband, promotion, and material things), but prayer in thankfulness and gratitude. While you're praying, pray for strength in times of weakness. Pray for protection in times of danger. Pray for guidance when you need direction. Pray for peace in times of turbulence. Pray for love in times of heartache. Pray for fortune in times of misfortune. The old folks used to call it being "prayed up." When you're prayed up the Spirit hears your prayers, so that while you're sitting at that red light and a car runs it, your prayer for protection tells you to sit there a little longer and you do it without knowing why. You just listen to that something "The Spirit" and you sit there protected from danger and harm's way.

Listening to your Spirit is the beginning of understanding. Once you understand how life works you'll make wiser decisions and therefore wisdom will be your guide. Think about it, sisters!!!

SISTERS DYING OF AIDS

African-American women (sisters) are dying of AIDS faster than any other group of people. The latest statistics still show (us) being infected with HIV and AIDS in growing numbers each time the report from the CDC is released. What's so puzzling about this entire epidemic is that statistics also show that African-American women are the largest single-family group and least likely to get married and stay married. That means that the majority of us don't have a husband and are not in a monogamous relationship. Rising numbers of single black women hold down various positions throughout Corporate America, the entertainment industry, politics, and in education, and single black women are becoming entrepreneurs, owning daycare centers, beauty and nail salons and other businesses. However, in all of our independence, financial success, raising our children alone, overcoming obstacles, we are dying of AIDS. Why is that? Could it be that we're not listening to the reports, the commercials, not learning to practice safe sex? Or, are we so busy trying to overcome, succeed, and find a good man, that we've turned a deaf ear to reality?

Let me paint a picture of reality for you, sisters. If African-American women are dying in record numbers from AIDS, and our men are dying from crack, being killed, and jailed, where does that leave the African-American race? Extinct, non-existent in just a few short years.

AIDS is unlike any other disease such as diabetes, cancer, obesity, heart disease and other hereditary illnesses that make up our genetic DNA. AIDS is 100% preventable, maybe not curable but definitely preventable. There's always exceptions to the rule such as rape, blood transfusions, accidents; however, contracting AIDS through sexual intercourse is 100% preventable.

Sisters, I've said it before and I'll say it a thousand times, WE HAVE SO MUCH POWER! We don't have to die of AIDS or become victims of other sexually transmitted diseases or have unwanted pregnancies that lead to unwanted children or abortions. We have the power and it's our bodies. Learning self-love and respect is the beginning to the end of this deadly disease. Making wiser decisions about who we give ourselves to so freely is the next step. In our search for Mr. Right, we've got to learn patience, pray and surrender our wills to The Almighty. Using sex as a tool for physical pleasure or to find a good man is not the answer. It doesn't matter how good we look, or how good the men look, we need to understand that our lives are on the line when we have unprotected sex and sleep with men whom God didn't send to us. And most of the men, 99.9% of them, are not God sent. A God sent man will have God like qualities and sex will be the last thing he wants. Time is a factor in determining if someone is right for us, and in time, if we wait, God will reveal to us everything we need to know about him, good and bad, and that alone will be enough to make a commitment or not. Sex is not the answer to finding a good man. Think about it, sisters!!!!

WHERE THE SPIRIT LIVES. . . .

Where is God? Is He/She in the heavens, the universe; where is that sacred place that the Omnipresent resides? How is it that He/She is always near and present in times of trouble? Is He/She in the Temple, Church, Mosque, Kingdom Hall, that place of worship, that sacred place? A place filled with holiness, cleanliness and divine consciousness. Where is that sacred place?

Well, the answer to those divine questions will surprise some and comfort others. God does not dwell in an unclean temple. Unclean means a place of lust, greed, jealousy, hatred, fornication and adultery. The Spirit of God resides in you, your body, your temple, only if the above-mentioned iniquities don't reside in you.

The Spirit of God is with us at all times watching, protecting and guiding us, although the Spirit may not actually reside in us because our temples are not clean, sacred. Our bodies (male, female) should be temples of God, places where the Spirit lives. However, the evil spirit deceives us constantly through temptation and our human weaknesses; therefore, the Spirit flees and when that happens it causes our bodies illness, and disease.

When the Spirit resides inside us it shows on the outside, in the way we speak, our gestures and our consciousness towards others. Our spirits will be humble, our dispositions meek and compassionate. Our acts of kindness will overflow and we will not yield to the wiles of the devil, the temptations of life, lust, and all of the negative spirits in the universe.

Having a humble spirit means not being boastful, harsh or superior in any way. It means giving praise to God for all of the blessings that flow in our lives. One of the ways the Spirit lives in us is through celibacy. Celibate simply means "the absence of sex," for a period of time. Married couples should practice celibacy periodically to cleanse the soul, the temple so they (the couple) can get closer to God. Singles should practice celibacy as a way of life, abstaining from sex until God unites them with their spiritual mates.

In order for the Spirit to use us completely, our temple must be clean. Celibacy purges our bodies of its iniquities and provides clarity for discovering our life's purpose. Where the Spirit lives (our temple), there's joy, peace, happiness and love. Think about it, sisters!!

LIVING BY FAITH

Are you living by faith? The Bible states that faith is the substance of things hoped for evidence not seen. What does that definition really mean? The majority of us believe in God and belong to a church or religious organization and know how to pray. However, when it comes to having faith and exercising our faith, we lack the true courage and belief that our faith will sustain us.

When I quit my job, and stepped out on faith, I was told that I was crazy and that faith was not enough to pay my bills and take care of myself and my son. There were those who told me that God wants us to have faith but He would never tell anyone to quit their job. "God wants us to work," people said. My Pastor even said, "You have to crawl before you walk," and I thought, well I've been crawling all of my life, it's time for me to get up and run. I couldn't believe the number of religious people who came to me with their fears, and when I told them I had faith and was doing what God told me to do, they didn't believe that faith was enough to live on. I found out that faith is something that we all know the definition of, but true faith is what most of us lack.

Faith-- the substance of things hoped for evidence not seen
    substance -material, element, spirit
    hope - to wish for with expectation, to desire
    evidence - signs or facts on which a conclusion
    can be based
    seen - (see) to perceive with the eye

Faith really means to expect or desire something when the signs or facts can't be seen with the eyes. That's why it's called blind faith, because what you expect can't be seen. So how many of you really live by faith? We have faith in that which is tangible and visible. We have faith in our jobs, credit cards, bank accounts, husbands, boyfriends, and preachers. Our faith depends upon that which can be counted, touched or seen. We believe and praise the Lord for our jobs, cars, homes, all of which are based on money.

There were only a hand full of people that told me that my faith was all that I needed and most of those people had already stepped out on their faith and found success doing what God told them to do. Blind faith is what we're going to need in the 21st century. With most of the major companies downsizing, crime out-of-hand, and our children growing up in this cruel world, it's going to take blind faith to live. Exercising blind faith and living by faith will require re-prioritizing our lives. Because we put so much value in material possessions and false beliefs, we've lost our faith. Are you living by faith? Think about it, sisters!!

SPIRITUAL BEAUTY

As women, most of us spend an enormous amount of time making sure we're physically beautiful. Society dictates to us what beauty is or should be. We're determined to be the perfect height, shape and size, wear the latest designer clothes and buy the finest material things. There's very little effort put into spiritual grooming. Just think what the outcome might be if we spent as much time grooming our spirits, our souls, as we spend in the beauty and nail salons and shopping. The one thing that's so wonderful and powerful about spiritual grooming is that Calvin, Donna, Tommy, Boss, Guess, and MAC, have no fashions, designs or makeup that can beautify your spirit. Spiritual beauty comes from the one and only designer, The Almighty.

Spiritual grooming requires time alone, to think and soul search. It means taking inventory of your personal life and determining what's wrong and right about one's self. Having a beautiful spirit surpasses physical beauty because your soul won't require acceptance from society, but assurance from God that you are His unique creation, therefore, BEAUTIFUL!

When your spirit is beautiful, kindness, love, compassion and understanding are your wardrobe of choice. Giving, sharing, teaching, reaching are your daily accessories and makeup. Your warm smile, gentle touch, positive attitude and humble disposition are your appeal. With your spiritual beauty, God's beauty, you'll attract other God-like spirits in your relationships with people.

Until we learn to spiritually groom ourselves, we'll always be unhappy with ourselves, and always attract negative spirits to us, and continue to have unsatisfying relationships in our lives. Think about it, sisters!!

THE GARDEN OF LIFE

In the garden of life, are you a flower or a weed? Like any garden, in order for the flowers to grow, the weeds have to be removed. A flower starts out as a seed and when planted it has to be watered and cultivated before it blossoms to its full beauty. It needs nurturing and pruning and the weeds grow without being planted. Weeds automatically grow and can hinder the flowers' growth if not removed. Weeds block the sun and grow close to the root of the flower, soaking up its water and nutrition. The gardener has to tend to the garden on a regular basis and pull the weeds out so that all the flowers can blossom and bring beauty to the garden.

Our lives work on the same basis as the flowers. If you're a flower, God has planted the seeds for your life, and while you're blossoming the weeds get in the way. The weeds are negativity, doubt, fear, and hatred among other things. Those weeds are usually the people close to your roots. They block the sun and soak up your water and nutrition. While you're busy trying to blossom, the weeds are constantly growing. When you look around they're everywhere and you have to pray to the gardener to remove the weeds so that you can grow.

Before a flower reaches its full bloom, the gardener has removed all of the weeds. The bulb of the flower starts to lift up and opens its petals and stands at attention. Its beauty is complete, its petals outstretched, and it looks like it's giving praise. All of the flowers in the garden seem to blossom at the same time and when they look around they see all of the other different flowers and together they bring beauty to the garden and all of the weeds are gone.

If you're a flower you may be blossoming, and while you're growing you may seem to be losing your friends and family and don't understand why. God is doing some weeding in your life. He's removing all of the weeds in your life in order for you to blossom. Once you've blossomed you'll meet other flowers that have been growing in the garden with you. You'll discover that all of the weeds that were once close to your roots are gone, and the garden of life is complete and full of flowers of all different breeds and colors and together they make life beautiful. Everyone loves flowers they represent beauty and God's love. In the garden of life are you a flower or a weed? Think about it, sisters!!

LIVING BY DEFAULT

*"A life without commitment and dedication
is a life without purpose"
-Anfra*

Do you live a pro-active or re-active life? Many of us may not know or understand the difference? Living a pro-active life means being in control of our daily lives. Being pro-active simply means planning, scheduling, budgeting and being prepared and committed to living life to the fullest. Being re-active means just the opposite. Instead of planning, scheduling, and budgeting, etc., you live life totally re-acting to the different situations and circumstances that happens in our lives each day. For example, a pro-active person plans to take lunch each day and maybe only eats out once a week, and a re-active person makes no plans for lunch or dinner and ends up eating out everyday and over-spending because there's no budget to follow for the week.

A person with a pro-active life usually makes commitments to exercise, participate in church programs or other extra-curricular actives such as involvement in the community or continuing education. In order for your life to have purpose, there has to be a plan and schedule to follow and above all commitment.

34

If you're a person that reacts to everything, there's no structure to your life. Each day is open for anything to happen. Therefore you have no plans to follow, no schedules to meet and no commitment to help others or further your education. You're living by default when you're reactive. There's no control and daily routine other than your daily work schedule.

Living in a re-active mode can be hazardous to our well-being because it leaves us open to unwanted spontaneity. We make spontaneous decisions that affect our health and finances. Being re-active causes stress that leads to other health issues such as obesity and high blood pressure.

Being on purpose requires commitment and dedication, having a plan and executing that plan. When you're pro-active you're on purpose because you have time to listen and obey what God has planned for you.

We all should focus on getting our lives in order and on purpose, and we can start by being pro-active. We can start by planning what to wear each day and what to eat for lunch and dinner. Each small plan that we make eliminates the last minute decisions and allows us time to do something positive for ourselves and others. Think about it, sisters!!!

MAYBE GOD'S TRYING TO TELL YOU SOMETHING

Are you trying to find happiness, joy and peace in your life? You thought you'd find it when you got that promotion on your job. You put in all the long hours and went that extra mile, gave 110% and finally after being passed up over and over again you got it. Striving for that promotion was your idea of happiness and success and would finally validate you as a person. What you find out oh to soon is that you're still empty, working even longer hours and giving more than 110% just to prove you deserved the promotion. **MAYBE GOD'S TRYING TO TELL YOU SOMETHING!**

Maybe you feel a need to lose weight, dye your hair or get a make over in order to be happy. You constantly shop and buy the latest designer clothes, dine at the finest restaurants, but when you come home, hang up your new wardrobe and look in the mirror, you're still empty. You're still searching and not satisfied with the new and improved look. **MAYBE GOD'S TRYING TO TELL YOU SOMETHING!**

The relationship you're in gives you physical satisfaction and pleasure and keeps the loneliness away, but deep down inside you know you're living a lie. You're involved with the wrong man and just don't know how to let go. He keeps telling you that he loves and needs you, but your heart is empty and your spirit's weak. You're always trying to justify your relationship with him. **MAYBE GOD'S TRYING TO TELL YOU SOMETHING!**

36

In order to find happiness, joy, and peace the first thing to do is *GIVE UP*! Yes, surrender your will to God totally. Accept who you are and where you are and be happy. Happiness is not a pursuit, a constant need to change, grow, elevate or consume. Happiness is a "state," a consciousness and awareness of the presence of God in your life. Joy and peace are sister and brother to happiness, love is the mother and God is the father. God loves to give you happiness, joy and peace! Until we learn to first honor and obey our Father, we'll forever be in constant pursuit of happiness and endlessly feeling empty and unsatisfied with our lives.

Maybe God's trying to tell you, "Seek ye first the kingdom of heaven and all things will be added unto you." Maybe God's trying to tell you, "He who finds a good woman has found a good thing," or maybe just maybe, God's trying to tell you, "Charm is deceptive, beauty is fleeting, but a woman who fears the Lord is to be praised." **MAYBE GOD'S TRYING TO TELL YOU SOMETHING?** Think about it, sisters!!

CUSSIN' & FUSSIN'

Not long ago I found myself in a temporary financial situation... I was broke. My check was supposed to have been automatically deposited into my account on Wednesday. However, that Thursday morning I got up to take my son to school and to leave for work, stopped by the ATM machine to get some cash, and my account had a zero balance. Now I thought something was wrong so I tried again at another ATM machine - same figure, zero balance. Well, I was driving on "e" and had to drive twenty miles to get to work and twenty miles home, plus I was already running late as usual. I prayed all the way to work, knowing there had to have been some logical reason that my check was not deposited and I would straighten things out with the bank when I got to work. I called and was told that my check had not been deposited due to an oversight; they hadn't received it from my company. My company said they didn't get my time sheet from me on time, so whose fault was it? Mine. Needless to say, I was pissed with no one to blame but myself.

The drive home was horrible. I knew I didn't have enough gas to drive home and yet I had no cash or resources. On the way home I decided to drive through the city instead of the interstate, just in case I ran out of gas. Well, I caught every red light on the twenty-mile drive and I started cussin' and fussin' at the other drivers.

"Will you slow ass people please get outta my way," I said - to myself of course.

"Dammit light would you please change so I can get home!" I screamed.

I was just a cussin' and fussin' and it seemed that everyone knew I was about to run out of gas and was taking his time. My blood pressure was rising as I gripped the steering wheel with both hands and gritted my teeth. I was sweating bullets because it was hot outside and I had to drive with the windows down, but I was still cussin' and fussin' at myself for not turning my time in. My car started making a noise, like it was about to stop, so I stopped cussin' and fussin' turned the volume down on the radio, and started praying.

"Lord, help me please. Let me make it home, Lord. Help me," I prayed out loud. "Show me what to do. I have no money, no gas, please Lord." God said to me in that inner voice, "Pull over at the next gas station."

"Pull over at the next gas station!" I shouted. "Lord what part of this prayer don't you understand?" I said, "I don't have any money; you know, duckies, cheese, moola!!"

He said, "Pull over at the next gas station." Well, I've learned to listen to that inner voice, even though I thought it was crazy to pull up to a gas station without any money, but God told me to and I did.

39

You Are My Sister

Just as I pulled up to the pump, another car pulled up behind me and a sister got out. I looked at her through my rearview mirror and she was counting some ones in her hands as she got out of her car. God said to me, "Ask her for two dollars," and I did as I tried to explain my situation. She handed me the money before I could finish my explanation. She said, "Something told me to only get five dollars' worth of gas, not the entire seven I have in my hand." I knew immediately that something was God. I said, "God bless you, sister," and she smiled and said, "God bless you, sister." I paid for the gas and cried and prayed all the way home, no longer cussin' and fussin'.

How many times have we been in a situation or had a problem and God tells us what to do but it sounds crazy and we dismiss it? We end up with a bigger problem because we thought we could handle it ourselves.

As long as we're cussin' and fussin' God can't speak to us, but as soon as we start praying He gives us the answer and all we have to do is obey. Think about it, sisters!!

Anfra Boyd

PRAYING FOR RAIN

Are you experiencing a season of drought in your life? Does everything in your life seem dried up: your bank account, job, joy, happiness and sex? Are you praying for rain and asking God to hurry up and send you some relief? As the days, weeks, months and maybe years pass you're beginning to wonder if God is even hearing your prayers. The foundation of our very lives needs watering in order to blossom, prosper and survive. This season of drought in your life has you feeling destitute and empty.

Iyanla Vanzant says, you're in the "meantime" when there's a drought in your life. It's what you do in the meantime that prepares you for the rain. While you're in the meantime, however, the devil hears your prayers, and intercepts, sending you a drizzle, sprinkle or slight shower, something temporary to deceive you.

While you're in the meantime it may seem like a lifetime or a long time before the rain comes. We have to remember that in the meantime God is on time and no matter how long it takes, if we have faith, be patient and continue to pray, when the rain comes it will be on time.

When praying for rain we should get prepared. Take out the umbrellas, raincoats, boots and buckets. We should exercise our faith, be patient and God will open up the windows of heaven and pour us out a blessing. He'll rain down on our lives and our buckets will overflow. Our lives will be renewed and we'll blossom and prosper in abundance.

So while we're in the meantime and experiencing a season of drought, and a drizzle or slight shower shows up, some temporary relief, don't be fooled into thinking it's a blessing from God. When praying for rain we should wait for rain. God is not a temporary God. What He gives and does is everlasting. The temporary relief in our lives only makes the drought even longer, the need more painful and prolongs the rain. Are you praying for rain? Think about it sisters!!

WHAT'S BLOCKING YOUR BLESSINGS?

Sisters, what's blocking your blessings? Is it the relationship you're in? Is it your job or your family and children? What is it that's blocking your blessings? The answer to these questions will probably surprise most of us. Most of us probably feel it's the relationship we're in. We're either dating a married man, married to the wrong man, or involved with the wrong man period. Some of us may feel it's our job that's blocking our blessings. The constant corporate shuffle where we're either not qualified or over qualified to get to the next level of management. For others it may be our families and children that are blocking our blessings. It may seem that our jobs are never done because we're trying to please everyone and make sure the household is up to par, that the children have the latest and greatest video games, designer clothes and expensive tennis shoes, and of course, keeping our husbands satisfied sexually. At the end of the day there's not enough time left to just relax, meditate, and spend some time alone doing something that calms our spirits and nourishes our souls.

For those of you that feel it's your relationship that's blocking your blessings, ask yourself a few questions. Why am I in this relationship? What is this man doing for me that God can't do? Answer these questions openly and honestly and write the answers down and read them daily.

Unless your man is holding a gun to your head and holding you hostage, he's not blocking your blessings. No matter how wrong the relationship is, if he's married, or you're married to the wrong man, or whatever the situation may be, there's nothing blocking your blessings but YOU! Of your own free will you've decided to date or marry a man that's wrong for you. And of your own free will you've decided to stay in the relationship with him; therefore, the blessings that God has for you are shortened or cut off. God cannot use you completely and openly bless you unless you surrender your will to Him completely.

If it's your job that you feel that's blocking your blessings, you may feel trapped because the company provides good health insurance, retirement benefits, and of course a 401 (k), and all of your credit cards are probably charged to the max. You probably see no way out or up; therefore, instead of making plans and setting goals in order to advance your career, you get deeper in debt trying to buy happiness. So who's blocking your blessings? YOU ARE!

Our families are very important in our lives; we need them and they need us. However, we must learn to prioritize and delegate the responsibilities of the household to our husbands and children. We should make the time for God and ourselves a priority in our lives.

Making time for God requires spending time alone with our spirits. We need quiet time to pray and meditate, to gain strength to be good wives, mothers, sisters and friends. You are the only one that's blocking your blessings when you try to satisfy everyone else's expectations and needs and neglect your own spiritual needs.

You are the only one that's blocking your blessings. We're all on a spiritual journey to peace and happiness and in order to get there we must first learn to do what's best for us spiritually. There's no excuse that's acceptable, no reason to not evaluate our lives and the relationships we're in and decide to change or correct the areas that are not pleasing to God. God has a blessing in store for all of us, and He's ready and waiting to open up the windows of heaven and pour them out. All we have to do is get prepared by moving the stumbling blocks in our lives. Think about it, sisters!!

FROM POWERLESS
TO
POWERFUL

Until recently, I'd been living my life powerless, unhappy and without purpose. I prayed and asked God to show me what He wanted me to do, to use me. First I became celibate, not knowing that that was the beginning of great things to happen in my life. I was sick and tired of being sick and tired and stressed all of the time. I kept being sick and the doctors couldn't heal me because there's no medicine to cure stress. I was told to find a way to eliminate the stress in my life, and my job was the stress factor. I prayed for an answer and God told me to type up my resignation and I did.

I walked into my manager's office with revolution in my blood, fire in my eyes, and conviction in my heart that I was going to be free of the corporate shackle around my neck. A shackle that was choking the very life out of my spirit and soul.

I walked into his office with a letter of resignation stating that I was resigning to work for myself as an inspirational speaker and author. He looked at it first before reading it, because it was typed on my own letterhead.

"Oh, so you're quitting," he said. "Why? You're not happy here? I see you want to be a writer huh. I didn't know you had any talent." I held my breath before answering.

"You only see me eight hours of the day. I do have a life," I responded.

"Do you have to quit in order to write and speak?"

"Yes, I do."

"Why?" he questioned.

"Because as long as you and this company control my income, you control my life. You control where I live, what kind of vacation I can take and when. You control where I can send my child to school. I can longer live like that."

He saw the look of revolution on my face and conviction in my voice as I spoke. His face turned beet red, the same color as his Polo shirt. I assumed this was the first time that he'd ever seen a Black woman take control of her life and he was speechless. He stood and shook my hand nervously and said, "I hate you're leaving. You've been a good employee."

I walked into his office a powerless employee and I walked out of his office a powerful entrepreneur. I walked out on faith, determined that no "white" man or any man would ever have power in my life again. I wanted to enter the new millennium with a plan, a purpose and power. Hallelujah!

Sisters, there's a revolution going on. We can no longer be powerless in our own lives. We have to make the transition from powerless to powerful in order to find purpose and peace in our lives. We can do this by breaking the shackles that hold us down. We're shackled in debt, shackled in bad relationships, shackled in corporate bondage, and shackled to society's standards of what we ought to be. In order to be what God wants us to be, we have to be free.

As the new millennium rapidly approaches, let's enter it together as powerful sisters. Sisters that have strength to climb the highest mountain. Let's help each other reach our dreams. Let's learn to pray together and honor and respect each other. Let's leave behind the shackles of the twentieth century and soar to greatness as *Powerful Women in the New Millennium!!* Think about it, sisters!!!

YOU ARE *"POWERFUL"* MY SISTER!

Anfra Boyd

LIVING YOUR DREAMS

Are you living your dreams? What is it that you dream of having, doing or being? Why is it called, "Living Your Dreams?"

A lot of sisters have written me asking how to find their purpose in life. Finding your purpose in life is not a search outwardly; instead, it's an inward approach. No one has the answers to your purpose in life. Your purpose is deeply rooted in your dreams. In your dreams lie the answers, desires, skills and talents needed to do your life's work. While in your dream state, the Divine Spirit speaks to your human spirit and reveals to you your purpose in life. Sometimes those dreams may seem far-fetched from the reality of the person you are everyday. Interpreting those dreams is sometimes difficult because most of us are taught to be what our parents wanted us to be and what society dictates we should be. The reality is, we should be what God intended for us to be.

For over twenty years I dreamt periodically of seeing myself speaking in front of a large crowd of people. In the dreams people were shouting, clapping and saying Amen. I would start running in the dreams because I knew that couldn't be me because I was very shy. I would wake up out of breath with my heart beating fast and frightened of what I had seen in my dreams.

Over ten years ago I found myself testifying at a church service where I was visiting with a friend. I didn't plan to testify because I was still shy, but the Spirit moved me to speak. During my testimony I noticed people shouting, clapping and saying Amen just like in my dreams.

Since then, whenever I speak people are always shouting, clapping and saying Amen and I'm no longer shy and very comfortable speaking in front of a large crowd. My dreams are no longer dreams but a reality of who I am, my purpose fulfilled and my spirit set free.

Until you decide either consciously or subconsciously to live your dreams there will always be a void in your life. Nothing will fulfill your spirit and soothe your yearning. Finding your purpose and doing your life's work unlocks the keys to abundance. You'll have an abundance of joy, happiness, peace and love while doing your life's work. The universe will answer your call and bring to you everything needed to live abundantly and do your life's work. Health, wealth and prosperity will overflow in your life.

Your purpose in life won't require man's approval, authority, degrees, ordaining, reviewing or opinion. You'll be qualified to do your life's work with the God-given talents that you already have. The only requirements that God has is that you: live by faith, be obedient, listen to His voice and do His will in your life. That's the spiritual formula for finding your purpose and living abundantly.

As you begin to do your life's work you'll discover the beauty of the universe and start to appreciate the smallest things. You'll start to view life so differently and discover talents that you never thought you had and those talents will help you become successful.

Finding your purpose in life is finding peace and it starts in your dreams. Are you living your dreams? Think about it, sisters!!

WEIGHT PROBLEMS

Do you have a weight problem? I do. Most of us are battling a weight disorder in our lives. No matter what shape or size or what the scales read we're never happy with our current status. We're either too tall or short, not enough breasts or butt or too much. We never look in the mirror and feel totally confident about ourselves. We're constantly comparing ourselves with women in the magazines or fashion models. Society has painted a picture of what a beautiful woman looks like physically and we've accepted that image and try desperately to fit that mold. There's so much focus and consciousness on weight issues that we've lost sight of what's truly weighing us down.

Our weight problems stem from being heavy burdened spiritually, financially and emotionally. In order to become physically fit, first we have to focus on being spiritually fit. Our spirits need nurturing and stimulating. Learning self-love and self-respect are key factors in becoming spiritually fit. Reading, long walks, meditating, and spending time alone help to develop spiritual growth and awareness. Eliminating negative thoughts, people and situations help our spirits awaken, causing our minds to focus on what's needed in our lives to succeed and become healthy.

We spend more time rushing to and from work, school, church and other places and never really slow down to think healthy thoughts. In our different religious activities we spend so much time going to and from church. There's always rehearsals, meetings, Sunday School, Bible Study and other church-related events that we tend to forget that we're supposed to grow and live spiritually. There's no spiritual purpose or gain in most of the activities that we participate in; therefore we're left empty and exhausted instead of being spiritually uplifted. Our spirits are heavy burdened and need daily nurturing and stimulation in order for us to move to a higher level of spiritual living.

Our financial burdens are weighing us down also. If you're like me, you rob Peter and all of his family just to pay Paul, and when it's time to pay Peter you rob Paul and all of his family to pay Peter back. You know the financial shuffle we all go through; write a check to cover a check that you wrote yesterday and you end up going to the bank daily to make deposits to cover the checks so they won't bounce and before you know it it's payday and you start all over again. Financial burdens cause mental and spiritual stress and most of us live pay check to pay check without ever stopping to realize that we're only getting deeper and deeper in debt.

We've got to learn to live practically and on a budget in order to lift the heavy burden of debt. Materialism and greed are two of the most common reasons we're in so much debt. Financial planning, budgeting and self-control will help to eliminate our debts and free us of worry and stress, allowing us to use our resources to reach a higher level of financial freedom.

Emotional burdens are the most deadly weights that we carry. Unhappiness on our jobs, with our families and the relationships we're in, cause emotional disorders that have an affect on our bodies. Emotional burdens can cause obesity, alcoholism, drug abuse and compulsive behaviors such as gambling, which can become addictive and detrimental to our well-being.

Then there's another weight problem that most of us have; we're waiting to lose weight, waiting for our children to grow up, waiting to find a man, or waiting to make more money, before we decide to live a more spiritual and healthy lifestyle. We're waiting on some miraculous event to happen that will change our lives instead of making our lives better ourselves each day that we live.

Freeing ourselves of the heavy burdens we carry is the first step to living a healthy and spiritual life. Our weight problems are killing us and we're dying a slow death. Free yourselves of your weight problems. Think about it, sisters!!!

FORK IN THE ROAD

On the highway of life, have you come to a fork in the road? While traveling life's highway you've run into many detours and bumps, maybe even ditches, trying to reach your destination of happiness and peace. Some of us are in the fast lane trying to reach happiness. We're using our bodies as vehicles and driving sex like a two-seater and end up spinning our wheels because the passengers we pick up are merely hitchhikers only needing a ride to their next stop. In the fast lane there's drugs, alcohol, sex, and money and we're in for the joy-ride until something unexpected happens like AIDS, addiction and abuse.

Some of us are driving in the middle lane and driving the speed limit. We obey all the rules and regulations of life's highway; we believe in God, pay our tithes, get educated, get a good job, take care of our families, yet we haven't reached happiness and don't understand why. We're so comfortable driving the speed limit that we're on cruise control until our lives are detoured by corporate downsizing, cut-backs, and layoffs.

Most of us are driving in the slow lane of life and don't try to speed up or take control of our destinies. We are accidents waiting to happen because everyone is trying to run us over trying to pass and out-do each other. In the slow lane is   fear, low self-esteem, inadequate jobs and housing and we accept the slow pace of life and live each day longing for a change of speed but we're afraid to accelerate. We're afraid of being rejected and/or left powerless in our own lives.

Finally we come to a fork in the road where there's no detour signs, no right turn only, no merging signs and no traffic lights. We must decide what road to choose and we're stuck in the middle, not knowing where each road leads. Down one road there may be job security, benefits, retirement, and health insurance. As you look down that road you can see your life and where you could end up. You can see, employment, a savings account, educating your children, and buying a big home. But what you can't see is peace, happiness, joy and love. When you look down the other road you don't see much; there's no job, no benefits, no big home, but you see a small light, a light that guides you to peace, happiness, joy and love. That light is drawing you, changing you, but you may be afraid because you can't see what it has to offer.

You Are My Sister

When you're at a fork in the road in your life, the decisions may seem hard and you're tired of the long road you've been traveling. You may be tired of bad relationships, drugs, alcohol, or maybe you've lost your job, or maybe you're tired of minimum wage and inadequate housing and you need to change directions.

Always remember that the road that you can see down the road of life, is not the road to choose. That road may be tempting and has all the material trappings but what you can't see is the heavy burdens you must carry down that road. The road of Faith is a road less traveled, but that's the road to choose in order to reach happiness and peace. That light you see down the road of Faith is God and He's guiding you, therefore you'll be safe and your spirit will be free. Think about it, sisters!!

SECRETS MAKE YOU SICK

I was recently talking to a fellow writer who has finished writing her autobiography titled, "Diaries of a Butterfly," and I asked her what made her decide to expose all of the secrets of her former lifestyle. Her simple reply was, "Secrets make you sick and I was tired of being sick." Those words stayed with me all during our conversation and I thought of my own secrets and how they have affected my entire life. Secrets are like cancer, eating away at our souls, causing our spirits to be terminally ill. Secrets eat away at the core of our being, eating away truth, honesty, respect, dignity, and love. Our deep dark ghosts of the past or our invisible lives that we live sicken our minds, bodies and spirits.

Secrets make you sick when you've been molested and abused as a child by your father, brother, uncle or close family member and were told by your abuser, "What goes on in this house stays in this house." Those family secrets of abuse never go away and leave us scared for life and living in constant fear of our past.

Secrets make you sick when you've been hiding a secret part of your life from your family and friends, living one life in the day time and another life at night. The mask of deception destroys our daily lives when we pretend to be something that we're not. We try to hide the shame and disgrace of being addicted, a prostitute or homosexual.

Secrets make you sick when you've been living in a tangled web of lying and cheating because the man you're in love with is married. The secret games of sex and betrayal haunt us when we have to meet at secret hide-a-ways, restaurants and motels. We're stealing love like a thief, breaking into our sister's life and taking her heart and trust and calling it our own. Those secrets destroy our integrity and self-respect and eat away at our hearts.

"The truth will set you free," is an old saying in the Bible, and one that couldn't be truer. Only in living a life of truth can we heal the cancer that keeping secrets causes. The truth, no matter what it exposes about us frees our spirits, lifting the heavy burdens of lying, deception and abuse.

My grandmother used to say, "Tell the truth and shame the devil," and I never really understood what she meant until I decided to tell the truth and live a life of truth. I realized that the devil uses the secrets in our lives to destroy us. Those secret skeletons in our closet of life hinder us from prospering and living abundantly. Secrets are kept quiet in the depths of our minds and creep into our lives each day and threaten to destroy us if exposed. The true secret is that if we expose those secrets the truth steps in and sets us free. We're free to fly like butterflies or soar like eagles and the secrets die and can no longer haunt or destroy our lives. Are you keeping secrets? Think about it, sisters!!!

GENERATION X

Our children, our young boys and girls, have become an endangered species. Society has labeled our babies Generation X. Some of us may think this label is appropriate, while others may not know exactly what the label really means. In Algebraic form the letter "X" means the unknown factor. To label something "X" means to eliminate, black out, cross out, destroy or kill. It also means dangerous and/or poisonous. Our children are being classified as the unknown, and targeted as dangerous and poisonous, therefore, X them out.

As I travel to our different schools and speak to our children, I'm saddened when I see them being disobedient, rude and dressed like a walking billboard for Tommy Hilfiger. Our boys have their pants hanging off their behinds and four or five gold teeth in what's called a "grill" on their front row of teeth. Our girls are dressed like the boys, gold teeth and all, and have four or five different hairstyles in one hairdo. Theirs names end in "esha," "quan,' "vante," and "eeka," and their attitudes are just plain ghetto-fabulous.

Generation X is our future and the most effective way to eliminate a race or group of people is to take away their future. Society is taking away our future and we're letting it. Everyday there are reports on the welfare system being eliminated and Affirmative Action being voted out in colleges and in the corporate world. The government is constantly raising the cost of a college education, while cutting back on grants and scholarships, and the average family can't afford to pay the high cost of a college education for their children. In the future fast food chains will require a bachelor's degree just to sweep the floor and flip a hamburger, and where will that leave our children? X'd out.

As parents we're contributing to the destruction of our own children- our future doctors, lawyers, astronauts, entrepreneurs and scientists. We've bought into the materialism that's ruining our children. We've lost our ability to parent by not teaching our children the love of God and how to honor, respect and obey. Their destruction is not totally society's fault. Each time we buy an expensive pair of Jordans', Tommy Hilfiger apparel and any other ridiculous designer brand or video game, we're taking money from our own children's future and investing it in someone else's.

We've given our children names that identify them as being "black" or from the ghetto. Their names alone will cause them to be discriminated against in the process of elimination for hiring. They've been taught that their God-given beauty is not beautiful or acceptable. Fake hair, and nails are worn to replace their natural beauty and elegance, and etiquette is a thing of the past for our young girls.

You Are My Sister

Most of our children don't have a spiritual foundation, and without the presence of God in their lives who will save them? Death and destruction are awaiting them. Drugs, alcohol, crack, AIDS and violence are waiting for the Generation X. Without a proper education and respect for the laws of the universe, death, hell or jail will be their home. Tommy Hilfiger won't save them, neither will Michael Jordan make that last-minute shot to save them. It's up to us as parents and a community to save our children from being X'd out. The next time you spend $60 for a pair of Tommy jeans, and $100 for a pair of Jordans', and then pay at least 21% interest on your credit card, think about your children's future. Hopefully you'll change your mind and invest your money in their education. Think about it, sisters!!

NOTHING'S PROMISED

Are you looking forward to retiring and moving to your dream home? Are you saving for that great age when you'll be debt-free and your children will be all grown up and the grandchildren can spend the weekends at your villa on an island somewhere? Most of us dream of retiring at an early age and traveling around the world, or spending quiet time doing the simple things in life. We're so busy planning or worrying about tomorrow that we forget about living in the moment. We act as if today doesn't count; only what we dream about tomorrow captures our hearts' desire. We dream of exotic vacations and romantic weekends and sleeping in late on rainy days because we will no longer have to work. We invest in 401(k) plans and have IRA accounts and pray that Social Security will be enough to live on when we retire.

A few days ago a former co-worker of mine was killed in a hit and run accident while crossing the street at her job. She was 55 years old and planning on retiring soon. I'm sure she planned on spending days with her husband playing golf on various golf courses around the country and traveling to Germany to see her grandchild a few times each year. Or maybe she was just planning on being home to cook dinner and make flower arrangements or participate in a local charity event.

During the past several years women close to me have died before reaching the golden age of retirement. Most of them died of some form of cancer and were not able to vacation or buy their dream home.

It didn't matter if they saved in a retirement plan or if Social Security would be enough to live on when they retired.

Nothing's promised in life and longevity is not ours to claim. Tomorrow belongs to God. "Give us this day our daily bread" is one of the lines in the Lord's Prayer. However, we don't understand what that prayer really means. God gives us each day to rejoice and be glad in it. Each day we should live in the moment and cherish it. We should cherish the time we spend with our families and treat our lives as if we've already retired. We don't have to wait to do the simple things, to smell the flowers and feed the birds and squirrels. And we don't have to be on an island to have an exotic and romantic vacation. When we awaken each day the beauty of the universe is at our disposal. The sun, moon, stars and all the elements of creativity are ours to cherish and rejoice in. God provides us daily with the things we need in order to live and be happy. He provides the bread (food) we need to eat, clothes to wear and gives us the beauty of creation to vacation in. We don't have to wait and plan to retire before experiencing the goodness that God has given us.

Nothing's promised and today could be your last day on earth. Did you stop to smell the flowers today? Did you tell your loved ones, "I love you," before saying good-bye? Did you take time to enjoy the sunshine or feel the raindrops on your face? Did you pay attention to the stars or watch the animals play? Why not? You're on vacation and tomorrow is not promised. Think about it, sisters!!

RELIGION & SPIRITUALITY

Religion has been part of our African-American culture since slavery. Our African ancestors practiced tribal rituals and believed in spirits. They considered the sun, moon, wind, rain, and all of the elements of the universe, as spirits. They prayed to these spirits for strength, guidance and protection. Native-Americans (Indians) also believed in spirits and practiced similar rituals as the Africans — praying to the spirits and naming their children after them or assigning one for protection.

After being captured and shipped to America, the Africans were taught to speak the "King James" English and were separated from others that spoke the same tongue in order to keep them from communicating with each other. As we all know, slaves weren't allowed to learn to read and write, but as time progressed they learned to read and write the "King James" English and also started to practice the white man's religion and read from his Bible. Before long their native tongue was lost and their beliefs faded and the practice of religion came into existence for them. Gone were their spiritual beliefs and rituals.

Today religion has so many divisions, denominations, and practices. Christianity is one of the leading religions accepted world wide -- the belief in Christ, the Savior, foretold by the prophets in the Old Testament. However, because of our religious beliefs, there's very little unity in Christianity. Our religion separates us: Catholic, Baptist, Methodist, C.M.E., A.M.E., M.B., Seven Day Adventist, Presbyterian, COGIC,

Church of God, Holiness Church, Jehovah's Witness, etc. Each denomination claiming to be the only way to be "saved" and follows their own doctrines, and worships under their own set of rules, all claiming to be led by God's holy word, the Bible. Because of our religion, we forget our Christian faith and spiritual purpose in life. We criticize, discredit, and downright hate each other's religion. In the name of the Lord we can't get along with each other and accept each other's faith. We argue and debate on what day of the week we should worship and what food we should or shouldn't eat and what name we should call the Holy One.

Spirituality differs from religion, because unlike religion where you go to a certain place, church, mosque, or temple to worship, spirituality is universal and not divided like religion. Being spiritual is a state of being and existence. Our African ancestors had it right when they believed that everything in the universe is a spirit. All of the elements, animals, and human beings are spirits and have a divine purpose in life, and that is to bring divine order and worship to the Holy One. Humans have strayed from their spiritual purpose in the universe. Religion and tradition have taken the place of spirituality and divided us into groups, classes, and color, which keep us from uniting together and loving one another.

In our religious teachings we're rarely taught the power we possess as spiritual beings. We're taught the stories of the Bible from Genesis to Revelations year in and year out, but rarely taught how to live each day in the Spirit. Living in the Spirit daily is a state of consciousness and awareness of the Holy Spirit within you, in your words, actions, gestures, and thoughts. As spiritual beings we have the power to speak life or death, abundance or poverty, sickness or health, into existence.

Being spiritual is unconditional and doesn't require laws, and doctrines, or certain days of the week to worship or serve. The universal laws of life guide you and protect you because you're on purpose, in divine order with the blueprint of God's plan for your life. Are you living in the Spirit? Think about it, sisters!!

THE SPIRIT OF TEMPTATION

Temptation is the desire to have or do something that's usually illegal or immoral. The evil spirit uses our weaknesses to tempt us and throw us off track, out of balance and away from the divine order of our purpose in life.

The temptation to steal is the most common of all, whether it's taking a pen or pencil from work, receiving too much money back at the grocery store or outright burglary or theft. Getting something for nothing and getting away with it is what tempts people to steal.

The temptation to lie and cheat is probably the second most common reason to yield. Lust, passion and attraction are a deadly combination when being tempted. The spirit of attraction causes us to lust for someone's physique. Lying and Cheating are partners in the game of temptation. They go hand-in-hand and you can't do one without the other. When lying and cheating the devil stacks the deck and uses sex as a tool of deception, wreaking havoc on our spirits and souls.

The spirit of addiction is the third and most deadly culprit in the trinity of temptation. As humans, we're naturally addictive. Our innate spirits desire love, compassion, and trust, among other things, and when left unfulfilled we seek out other elements to give us satisfaction. The spirit of addiction is usually dressed up in its royal attire and appeals to our senses.

In order to become addicted, the substance, i.e., love, drugs, alcohol, gambling, shopping, etc., either looks good, tastes good, or feels good, and comforts us temporarily. Once the sensation has departed, our mental psyche is on a mission to regain that feeling and we want or need more of the same; that's when the spirit of addiction captures us.

When you yield to temptation, the weakness of the flesh, you lose part of your virtue. Your spirit is raped if its divine connection to the Holy Spirit, leaving a hole in your soul. You lose patience, respect and dignity, all for instant satisfaction and gratification. Afterwards you're left feeling empty, because your spirit and soul are left naked and unprotected, and when that happens the consequences are detrimental to your purpose in life.

Do not yield to temptation the Bible says, one of the commandments we're to follow as God's law. However, we're constantly tempted each day and most of us yield to it in some form or fashion. It is when we learn to resist temptation that we start to understand our purpose in life and how living spiritually helps us to accept the responsibility for our actions and make wiser decisions when tempted.

They that wait upon the Lord shall renew thy strength and mount up with wings as eagles. Therefore, when you resist temptation, you soar like an eagle because your spirit's free. Think about it, sisters!!

THE SPIRIT OF JEALOUSY

The spirit of jealousy is an evil demon, a demon that lies dormant or mute as long as we're in despair, heartbroken or impoverished. Once the winds of change start to blow in our lives, the spirit of jealousy rears its ugly head. It shows up in our friends, family, co-workers, church members and even our spouses. Jealousy can be a doubled-edged sword in our lives; we can be jealous of others, and/or others can be jealous of us. Jealousy can cause us to envy each other's prosperity, success, joy and happiness. The spirit of greed is a partner of jealousy and together they can wreak havoc in our lives. The spirit of greed causes us to compete with others' material possessions and causes us to spend and consume at any cost to have more and out-do each other. The old cliché "Keeping up with the Jones'" is the philosophy of jealousy and greed and will cause emotional pain and put us in extreme financial debt.

Understanding the spirit of jealousy and greed can help us to remain focused and in control of our purpose in life. The fear of change causes us to become jealous of each other. Most of us fear growth, and in order to grow, a change has to happen. A change in thinking happens first. We start to think of ways that we can better our lives either spiritually, financially, and/or emotionally. Once the thoughts are processed, we then take action and action brings about a change. And that change of direction in our lives, which is usually an uplifting change, causes jealousy to show up in our lives through the people that we're close to. "I remember when," is a common statement and sign of jealousy in others.

78

A change in bad habits, bad relationships, bad attitudes, or a change in careers, among other things, causes others to say, "I remember when she used to...."

Jealousy weakens the spirit and causes conflict in relationships. The person prospering is weakened and left abandoned when jealousy rears its ugly head. The very friends and family that we thought we could count on in our success are the very ones who seem to show the least support. They often seem offended when others congratulate or mention our growth, change and success. The term, "fair weather friends" does not apply when jealousy shows up. Unlike fair weather friends who only want to be around when things are successful in our lives, jealous friends want no part of our success.

Conquering jealousy is a constant challenge for all of us. We must learn to support each other and remember the saying, "What God has for me is for me." With that understanding we can rejoice in the success of our family and friends. God is a good God and what He does for others He'll do the same for us. Knowing that should comfort us and help us to overcome jealousy. There's no measurement or competition when God blesses us. We should not covet our neighbors, family and friends. God blesses each of us in His own way and in His own time and we're blocking our blessings when we're jealous. Think about it, sisters!!

THE SPIRIT OF DISTRACTION

How many times have you been sitting in church trying to listen to the sermon, and you've gotten distracted? There's always that professional shouter shouting so loud that it keeps you from hearing and focusing on the message. You know the professional shouter; every church in America has at least one. He or she is normally the hell-raiser of the church and shouts louder than the Preacher and he's speaking into the microphone. Sister or Brother Professional Shouter/Hell-raiser shouts every Sunday like clockwork or like they're getting paid. Most of us just sit there mad, our spirits distracted and no matter how hard we try to focus on the message the shouter gets louder and louder. Sister or Brother Hell-raiser is trying to raise the dead, it seems.

Then there are the babies who sit quietly during service while the music is playing and the choir is singing, and as soon as the preacher starts delivering the message the babies join in with the professional shouter and everyone gets distracted. Heads start turning as the babies cry out loud and everyone's trying to determine what's wrong and asking themselves why won't the parents take the children out of the sanctuary? The professional shouter get louder and starts dancing and running while shouting, because the baby is getting too much attention. By now the whole church is distracted, even the preacher, who then says, "Can I get an Amen," and people say Amen, even though they really didn't hear a word he said with all of the distraction going on.

On your way to church you may get distracted by the smallest things to keep you from going or make you late. The phone rings just as you're on your way out the door, or company drops by, or you get caught by a train that takes forever to clear the tracks. There always seems to be some sort of distraction whenever there's something you need to hear from God.

The evil spirit uses the spirit of distraction at the most inopportune time — when there's a message that we need to hear from God. You're never distracted any other time. Even if it's not an external distraction like someone shouting, talking or crying, the spirit of distraction can be internal. Your mind could be a thousand miles away while sitting in service or when you need to pray. Usually your thoughts won't cease and your mind is constantly thinking about other things such as bill, lovers, sex, work or your children.

The spirit of selfishness is one of the ways that distraction rules. Selfish people don't care if you hear God's word. Their only concern is to be seen and heard and they have no consciousness or consideration of others. We tend to confuse their happiness and joy while shouting as the Holy Spirit overtaking them. The Holy Spirit is a humble spirit and would not make anyone so happy and joyful that it would keep others from hearing and receiving God's word. There are those times when we're truly thankful and joyful and express it by shouting and dancing; however that shouldn't happen every Sunday like clockwork with the same people each week.

Those people are pretentious and self-centered and usually ignorant when it comes to understanding the Humble Spirit of God.

Teaching and educating each other will help conquer the spirit of distraction. Our people need to be taught about humility and how to have compassion for others when in public places. We should understand that church is a public place, and when babies are crying and disorderly we should take them out to soothe, and/or discipline them. Everyone should be able to hear and receive the powerful message that God has given His ministers to uplift His people. Think about it, sisters!!

HOLY MATRIMONY
"I DO...DO I?"

"Do you take ____ to be your lawful wedded wife to have and to hold 'til death do you part?"

"Do you promise to love, honor and obey, forsaking all others, in sickness and in health?"

How "holy" is matrimony? Webster's dictionary gives the meaning of "holy" as sacred, and matrimony is "a lawful and spiritual union between man and woman." So, Holy Matrimony means a sacred, lawful and spiritual union between man and woman.

Marriage is the only union between man and woman that God sanctioned as holy and sacred. It is a union to be celebrated, and cherished when two people become as one. One faith, one love, one honor, one respect and commitment to obey the Higher Power, God.

In a time when the statistics for divorce are higher than ever before and single women are having children out of wedlock, and the world is being plagued by a sexually-driven disease, how important is saying, "I do"?

Let me pose a question, "If a man lies to God, his wife and family constantly time and time again and hurts the people he loves and holds dear to his heart, why wouldn't he lie to, about and with you?"

84

When saying, "I do":

Do I -- stand by my man over and over again and accept his games of lying and deceit?

Do I -- submit myself totally and face heartache and pain with a smile and under false pretenses?

Do I -- still feel compassion, trust and honesty for him?

Do I -- stay married for the sake of the children, family and others, although my heart is broken?

Do I -- keep forgiving and living with the one who robbed me of love, honesty and respect?

Do I -- stand up, speak out and walk away and never look back?

I do...do I? Sisters do you? I don't! Think about it!!!

WHY DO MEN CHEAT?

Well, ladies, here we are again with another leader apologizing for his sexual misconduct. Another politician, leader, man, human being, fallen. Our President's sexual misconduct is not new to the office or country; however in a time when the statistics for AIDS is growing faster by the day, you would think or expect our country's leadership — be it President, Politician, or Pastor-- would lead by example.

What is it about sex that renders humans powerless if given the right circumstances and opportunity? Why is it that we can make responsible decisions concerning matters of finance, health, career and parental issues, but to all "sex" is a weakness? What is about 15-20 minutes of physical pleasure (foreplay included) that makes us risk everything, our self-respect, love of God, family, career and reputation? All of these can be destroyed for a few minutes of physical pleasure. Is sex truly a human weakness, a matter of choice or a deception of (d)evil?

Sex in its natural state is a spiritual union shared between man and woman as husband and wife, a gift from God. God's gift was meant as a means for expressing love, and to reproduce, to be fruitful and multiply.

Its' been said over and over again that, "behind every good man is a good woman," and "the downfall of every good man is a woman." Therefore ladies, as women, we have SO MUCH POWER! So, to answer the age-old question; why do men cheat? because we (women) allow them to.

I've talked to so many women about the President's retraction, apology, admittance of his "inappropriate relationship", and 99% of the women said, "He's a man", "He's not the first President to sleep around." It seems to me that we, as women, as a nation, as a people, have accepted lying and cheating as a way of life, yet we complain about our men: the shortage of good men, men not being responsible, accountable, good fathers and husbands. Until women decide to step up to the plate and understand that we're part of the problem and also the solution to it, men will forever lie and cheat. We're part of the problem because we allow them to lie to us, for us and with us. We knowingly date them while they're married and accept their lies and disrespect God, ourselves and our sisters. We're the solution because we can make wiser choices and stop accepting anything less than what God wants for us. We can learn to practice self-love and self-respect, stand up for ourselves and stop letting men have power in our lives.

As for the President we have to forgive and move on and accept the lesser of the two evils and pray that this won't happen again, and it won't if women decide to seize their power. Think about it, sisters!!

THERE'S NO RIGHT WAY TO LOVE THE WRONG MAN

"**H**aving a man is better than being totally alone."

"I don't have a lot of time to put into a relationship anyway, with work, school and having a child."

"I don't need a man 24-7, let his wife or woman clean up and cook for him."

"He helps me pay my bills and gets my hair done."

"I can't find anyone else."

"He'll do until I find me a husband."

"Girl please, I can't stand being by myself. I gotta have man."

Sisters, how many times have we used or heard these excuses from women who are dating the wrong men? How do you know if he's wrong? If he's married, shacking, irresponsible, alcoholic, a drug addict, a drug dealer, abusive, and/or a liar, to name a few, he's wrong. Why do we try so very hard to justify dating the wrong man? Most of us don't look for or purposely date the wrong men. However, different situations and circumstances leaves us vulnerable and open game, prey for the wrong man.

Most of the time we find ourselves lonely, just ending a bad relationship, or needing financial help; that's when our guards are down, thus enters the wrong man in what seems like the right way. Our fear of loneliness is the main reason that we date the wrong man. We've been taught over and over again, that we must have a man to feel like a woman, to validate our femininity and our womanhood.

Dating on the rebound is another dangerous trap, because we're feeling empty, hurt and heartbroken and most of the time in need of attention and affection when Mr. Wrong approaches with his promises and good looks, satisfying our emotional thirst. Then there's money or the lack of, which depletes us of all moral thoughts and values. We need to put food on the table, shoes on Lil' Johnny's feet, gas in the car and of course, get our hair done, when Mr. Married man enters with his monetary help and stories, or rather lies, about his unhappiness with this wife.

Mr. Wrong is out there on the job, at the spa, grocery store, church, everywhere, waiting for the opportunity to prey on women who find themselves with their guards down. His approach is simple and unnoticeable. He shows kindness and understanding of our situation. His willingness to help or comfort and lend money sweeps us off our emotionally unbalanced feet. Before long we're caught up in the rapture with him and before we wake up, weeks, months, and years have gone by and we find ourselves trying to justify our relationship with him.

Women are no more than drug addicts when we date the wrong men, sprung on whatever it is that we think is good to us or for us. And just like a drug addict we can't let go because we're afraid of what might happen if we do. We're still searching for that first love, first high, good feeling or whatever it is that keeps us hooked on the wrong man. And he's no more than a drug dealer supplying us with the drug. Instead of crack, weed or alcohol, he's supplying us with money, lust, greed and sex, camouflaging it in the name of love and happiness.

No matter how much we say we believe and have faith in God when we're dating the wrong man, we're selling our souls to the devil and he's dressed up in a suit disguised as a man. We have to be strong and believe that there's nothing a wrong man can do or give us that God can't. Think about it, sisters!!

POETRY

BLESSED

When I think about my problems
my ups and downs and crazy turnarounds
and I'm feelin' a little depressed

I think of children starving, being abused
or having so much less
I realize that no matter what I've been through
My life has truly been
Blessed

When my heart is broken, and I'm feelin' sad and lonely
or under a lot of stress

I think about someone dying of AIDS
being in pain and feeling distressed
Within minutes I realize that through it all
My life has truly been
Blessed

When I feel that life has dealt me a terrible hand
I wanna give up 'cause I've had
more than I can stand, I realize that without me
how empty the world would be
for my child, my friends and my family

I realize that what I was feeling was only a test
To make me understand, that through it all
My life has truly been
Blessed

Anfra Boyd

AN ANGEL PASSED YOUR WAY

You never know who you might meet
As you're walking down the street
You never know as you go along each day
If one of God's Angels passed your way

So be careful as you speak and greet
You never know who you might meet
Say a kind word
Hello, Thank You or How was your day
That person might be a test
To see if you would turn
one of God's Angels away

All of God's Angels you might not recognize
They may need your help or support
They may ask you for money or to help with
their life's work
You may turn your back or not try to do your best
Believe me, God is putting you to a test

He's testing you each and everyday
To see if you are faithful and humble
To see if you would turn one of
God's Angels away

LIKE AN EAGLE

I SOAR LIKE AN EAGLE
FLYING HIGH AND ALONE
FOLLOWING MY DREAMS
AND NOT BOTHERING ANYONE

MY FRIENDS DON'T UNDERSTAND ME
'CAUSE I LIKE BEING BY MYSELF
I'M NOT DEMANDING OR SELFISH
JUST LOVING AND RESPECTING MY INNER SELF

WHEN YOU SEE ME FLYING HIGH AND FREE
I'M DOING THE THINGS THAT
GOD HAS PLANNED FOR ME

I DON'T LIKE BEING IN A GROUP OR
KEEPING UP WITH THE THINGS THAT ARE IN
I DON'T LIKE BEING PRESSURED OR
TRYING TO FIT IN

MY LIFE WAS DESIGNED TO BE FREE
LIKE AN EAGLE THAT'S ME
RISING ABOVE THE BOUNDARIES, LIMITS
AND EXPECTATIONS THAT OTHERS PLACE ON ME
FREE TO SOAR AND SPREAD MY WINGS
LOVING WHAT I DO AND LIVING MY DREAMS
LIKE AN EAGLE THAT'S ME
I'M FREE
FREE

Anfra Boyd

SOMEONE ELSE'S EYES

I've been trying to live my life
through someone else's eyes

Trying to be what everyone else wanted me to be

Trying to please my mother & father
Trying to be the perfect daughter

Trying to please and satisfy their lives
Living my life through someone else's eyes

Trying to be the perfect friend, sister, and mother
Trying to be the perfect girlfriend and lover

Trying to be what everyone else wanted me to be
Trying to please and satisfy their lives
Living my life through someone else's eyes

Trying to please and understand my man
Trying to be the perfect shape and size
Living my life through someone else's eyes

Now it's time for me to be
the beautiful woman God intended of me
No longer living my life full of lies
No longer living my life through

SOMEONE ELSE'S EYES

A MESSAGE FROM AN
UNBORN CHILD

PLEASE LET ME BE BORN
INTO THE WORLD CONCEIVED OF LOVE

BE CAREFUL AS YOU CHOOSE MY NAME
GIVE ME ONE THAT I'LL BE PROUD OF

DON'T LET ME BE BORN INTO THE WORLD ALONE
NOT KNOWING MY FATHER BECAUSE HE'S
ALREADY LONG GONE

DON'T BURDEN MY LIFE
WITH YOUR TROUBLES AND STRIFE
DON'T ABORT ME AND END MY LIFE

DON'T ABUSE YOUR BODY WHILE YOU'RE
CARRYING ME
I DON'T NEED ALCOHOL, CIGARETTES OR DRUGS
I NEED VITAMINS, NUTRITION AND LOTS OF
LOVE

I DON'T NEED DESIGNER CLOTHES
AND MATERIAL THINGS
TEACH ME TO LOVE, RESPECT, AND HONOR
ALL HUMAN BEINGS

Anfra Boyd

FILL MY LIFE WITH STRENGTH & DETERMINATION
I LOOK FORWARD TO A HIGHER EDUCATION

TOMORROW BEGINS A NEW LIFE FOR ME
I'M WAITING TO SHOW THE WORLD
THAT GOD HAS A PURPOSE FOR ME

SO TAKE CARE OF ME NOW
AND TOMORROW I'LL DO THE SAME FOR YOU
BECAUSE I AM YOUR FUTURE
AND WITHOUT ME THERE'S
NO HOPE FOR YOU!!

A MESSAGE FROM AN UNBORN CHILD

I GOT IT

THAT LOOK OF SUCCESS
THE WAY I WALK
AND THE CLASSY WAY I DRESS
I GOT IT

THAT FEELING U FEEL
WHEN U KNOW
YOU'VE BEEN BLESSED
I GOT IT

THE WAY I TALK AND THE WAY
I SAY WHAT I SAY
WHEN EVERYTHING IN LIFE
IS GOING MY WAY
I GOT IT

THAT FEELING OF JOY
EXCITEMENT & HAPPINESS
FEELING THANKFUL AND GRATEFUL
KNOWING IT'S ALL BY
GOD'S SWEET GRACE
I GOT IT

THAT LOOK OF STYLE AND FINESSE
THAT GOD-GIVEN
SEX-I-NESS
YES!!!
I GOT IT

BEAUTIFUL BLACK MAN

FROM THE TOP OF YOUR HEAD
TO YOUR FULL LIPS AND WIDE NOSE
DOWN TO YOUR BROAD CHEST AND BEAUTIFUL
MASCULINE FRAME
I LOVE EVERY PART OF YOU
MY BEAUTIFUL BLACK MAN

THE WORLD TRIES TO PUT YOU DOWN
MAKE YOU FEEL LESS THAN A MAN
LABELING YOU IRRESPONSIBLE, IGNORANT, AND
HAVING LITTLE CLASS
BUT THESE LABELS ARE GOING NO WHERE FAST

IT'S TIME FOR YOU TO RISE UP
AND TAKE A STAND SHOW THE WORLD THAT YOU
WERE CREATED BY GOD
AS THE FIRST STRONG, INTELLIGENT
BEAUTIFUL, BLACK
MAN

THE WAY YOU STROLL FROM SIDE TO SIDE
WHEN YOU WALK KNOCKS ME OFF MY FEET
THE WAY YOU CALL ME "BABE"
OOOH THOSE WORDS SOUND SO SWEET

THE DAY IS COMING FOR YOU
TO TAKE BACK YOUR REIGN
TAKE BACK YOUR PLACE IN
THE COURT OF LIFE
AS A STRONG & POWERFUL
BEAUTIFUL
BLACK
MAN

SEX & FRIENDS

When two close friends decide
to cross the line from friendship
to relationship normally the
friendship ends

Gone are the days of long
Heart-felt talks
and good old fashioned walks

Gone are the days of honesty and trust
the days and nights are now filled with
passion and lust

Once the relationship is over
and the sex ends
we must say good-bye to
what once was a
VERY CLOSE FRIEND

Anfra Boyd

SENSITIVE WOMAN

Do you wanna woman who knows where she stands?
A woman who's loving, affectionate and kind.
Do you wanna woman who can cook, run your bath water
and give a good message?
Do you wanna woman who can pay her own bills and still
give you chills?
Do you wanna a woman who's willing to give, you know a
woman who's sensitive?
Hell Naw!!
You wanna woman that's a size eight.
A woman like me you can't even begin to appreciate.
Do you wanna a woman who's just my size?
Hell Naw!!
You wanna a woman with 2" thighs
One that tells you plenty of lies
A woman that hangs out with Re-Re'em
A woman wearing heavy makeup, lots of weave and tight
jeans.
A woman with three kids by five different men.
A woman whose income the mailman brings.
Do you wanna a women like me that's sensitive?
Hell Naw!!!
You wanna a woman not willing to give.
A woman with 6" nails that gives you hell.
A woman that never calls and takes your money

You Are My Sister

and runs straight to the mall.
Do you wanna a woman like me that's a little thick?
Hell Naw!!!
You wanna a woman that treats you like one of her tricks.
'Cause sister's been with every Tom & Dick.
Do you wanna woman that treats you like a real man?
Hell Naw!!!
You wanna woman that never understands.
A woman who'll let you hit it and quit it and not be
committed.
A woman you have to chase and throws shit in yo' face
A woman who gives you plenty of drama and when she's mad
she talks about you and yo' mama.
Do you wanna woman like me that's sensitive?
Hell Naw!!
You wanna a woman that's a size eight
A beautiful black woman like me
you can't even begin to appreciate!!

Inspired by the Poem "Sensitive Man" by Eric
Melt The Mike Monday's in Memphis, TN.

Anfra Boyd

THE FINER THINGS IN LIFE

So you say you want the finer things in life
diamonds, pearls, expensive perfumes and furs
You're willing to rob, steal and kill
and cause so much trouble and strife
all because you want the finer things in life

Now you've made it over got a good job
credit cards, new cars and distinctly dressed
walking 'round proud with your head up
wearing some white mans' name on your chest
looking down on others and you think that's right
all because you have the finer things in life

So you say you want the finer things in life
you'll lie to your husband
cheat on your wife
everything you own is on your back
you want things so bad you'll even sell your brother crack

The finer things in life will drive you crazy, put you in debt
rob you of your pride and self- respect

To the devil you'll sell your soul
just to get out of the hole
and when it's all over you'll
want to end your life
all because you wanted
THE FINER THINGS IN LIFE

ANSWER THIS QUESTION

Do you believe that racism is still alive?

Do you believe that the white man
is still trying to keep us oppressed
through education, healthcare and
job opportunities?

Do you believe that prejudice
is at its highest level yet?

I can answer those questions for you
the answer is Yes.

Then answer this question
will someone please.

If racism is still alive and the white
man is still trying to keep us oppressed
and prejudice is at its highest level yet

Then there's something terribly wrong
something I don't understand
something I just can't figure

WHY IN THE HELL DO BLACK PEOPLE
PROUDLY WEAR CALVIN KLEIN, GUESS,
BOSS, AND TOMMY HILFIGER?

MS. CAINE

Hello ladies, my name is Ms. Caine
I just stopped by to let you know
that I want yo' man

One taste of my soft, sweet, sex appeal
will make yo' man rob, steal and kill

My lovin' is so good
that I can be found in every neighborhood

I just wanna let you know, tell you the signs
When your man starts coming home real late
don't think it's another woman
It just might be me a different kind of omen

No, now don't think I wanna take him from you or be his wife
He can have me any way he wants me
snort me, inject me or smoke me in a pipe
My only job is to take his life

My lovin' is much better than you giving him head
He won't stop loving me until he is dead

My name is Ms. Caine
and I don't play that
Brotha's gotta have some money
especially if he wants me
in the form of crack

Yeah, Ms. Caine's my name
and I'm one bad BITCH!!
I don't discriminate
don't playa hate

You better watch yo' man
when he starts coming home real late!

THUG IN A SUIT

Girlfriend don't be fooled by a brotha's
good looks and expensive suits
Brotha just might be a
Thug in a suit

Just 'cause he's not wearing
gold chains, diamond rings
and a gold tooth
Brotha just might be a
Thug in a suit

He may be wearing expensive
French cuff shirts and tailor
made suits, driving a Lexus
or Mercedes Benz, showing
off to all of his friends

Don't be fooled 'cause the brotha's
so damn sexy and cute
Brotha just might be a
Thug in a suit

Just 'cause he dresses so fine
and knows how to wine and dine
and looks like he may be President
or CEO of a Fortune 500 company

Brotha might not have a
legitimate J- O- B

So girlfriend don't be fooled by
a brotha's good looks and expensive suits
or because he's so damn sexy and cute
Brotha just might be a
Thug in a suit

TELL ME MR. PRESIDENT

Tell me Mr. President, why didn't you just say no?
No to your sexual desires and feelings
You of all people had the power to VETO

Tell me Mr. President, was your few minutes of
pleasure worth your lifetime of heartache and pain?
Was it worth ruining your reputation and American's good
name?

Tell me Mr. President, did you practice safe sex?
Did you use a condom or just say, "What the heck?"

Tell me Mr. President, did you sign the bill for gun control?
What you really needed, was to practice some self-control.

Tell me. Mr. President, just what laws did you pass,
while your pants were way down below your ass?

Tell me Mr. President, did you pass the bill against
Affirmative Action, while your lover was giving you
some satisfaction?

Anfra Boyd

Tell me Mr. President, I'm a black woman, a democrat,
I voted for you, I had your back.
Now you're acting like an alcoholic or a brotha on crack

Tell me Mr. President, do you need some sexual
rehabilitation?
Why didn't you learn from your past sexual connotations?

Tell me Mr. President, why did you lie and then take it back?
I'm sick and tired of men cheating and using the fact,
that they're only human or just a man, that's a poor excuse,
treating sex like alcohol or drug abuse.

Tell me Mr. President, do you know the latest statistics on
AIDS?
It just might be you ten years from now lying dead in your
grave, cause of death lying, cheating, heartache and AIDS!!

"TO THINE OWN SELF BE TRUE"

YOU ARE MY SISTER
PERSONAL INVENTORY

The next section is about
YOU!

The following pages are designed to examine the core of your being. There are personal questions, meditation, and how-to-lists on finding your purpose and growing spiritually. Please answer the questions openly and honestly and in doing so you'll find out information about yourself that you might not have known or even thought about. The questions are simple and the answers are life changing and only you can answer them correctly.

THE POWER OF MEDITATION

What is meditation? How is it different from prayer? Meditation is the quieting of the inner Spirit — the ability to sit still and block out all thoughts, physical movements and external sounds while listening to your inner voice and speaking directly to God, human spirit to Divine Spirit. When you meditate your body is still, relaxed and motionless, your breathing slows down along with your heartbeat and you lose consciousness of your surroundings. Once the mind has surrendered its will to the Divine Spirit, you're totally connected and one with God. Your Spirit is then able to speak and you began to talk spirit to Spirit. You're able to thank God for all the blessings in your life. You can speak to your body and it listens and responds to your requests. The power to heal comes from meditating because your spirit becomes Divine and listens and recognizes the voice of God and obeys like the rest of the universe does when God speaks and orders the thunder and rain, or the stars to shine. Meditation is the only time when you're in complete harmony with the universe. It's the only aspect of life where you're totally awake, yet completely powerless. While in meditation the mind returns to its embryonic state, like an embryo in the mother's womb. It is in that state that an embryo is given its purpose, and we lose all recollection of our purpose at birth. Meditation is the most powerful way to find your way back to your purpose and to live in peace and complete harmony with the universe.

The power of meditation is practiced in most eastern religions and very few Christian or western religions teach it. Prayer is taught along with the Bible, but very rarely are we taught to meditate, especially in the African-American community. Prayer is very powerful and while meditating prayer is used, but unlike meditation prayer does not connect you totally with God. Prayer can be done at anytime or place and doesn't require total surrender of the mind, body and spirit.

Once the meditation is complete, the mind and body return to their normal state. Your spirit will be at peace and you're able to face each day with God's assurance. You'll feel compelled to live each day in the Spirit and you'll be able to listen and follow God's instructions daily.

MEDITATION PRAYER

(Find a comfortable place in your home, a scared place, and use it to meditate each day. Relax your body and start to breathe deeply, inhaling and exhaling with your mouth and eyes closed. I suggest burning candles as a symbol of freedom.)

Repeat these words until all of your thoughts are gone and your mind is totally quiet:

Ah...Ah..Ah-men.......Ah...Ah... Ah-men....Ah...Ah... Ah-men

breathe

Ah...Ah..Ah-men.......Ah...Ah... Ah-men....Ah...Ah... Ah-men

breathe

Ah...Ah..Ah-men.......Ah...Ah... Ah-men....Ah...Ah... Ah-men

relax and breathe

Ah...Ah..Ah-men.......Ah...Ah... Ah-men....Ah...Ah... Ah-men

Heavenly Father

I come to give thanks for another day
Thanks for the sunshine and the rain
Thanks for protecting me and my family
from danger
Thanks for health and strength and a sound mind
Father
I surrender my mind, body and spirit
to Your Divine Will
Please take away all that is within me
that is not of Your will
Take away cancer, diabetes, AIDS and
any other diseases
Take away all aches and pains and
give my mind and body peace
Father
Speak to me so that I may always hear
and follow Your commands
Father
Bless my finances so that I can provide for
my family and help others
Touch the world and bring peace to it

THANK YOU FATHER
AH...AH...AH-MEN
AH...AH...AH-MEN

SIGNS OF BEING SPIRITUALLY BANKRUPT

1. Do you shop impulsively most of the time?
   yes   **no**
2. Do you party at least once a week or more?
   yes   **no**
3. Are you not involved in a church or community organization?
   yes   **no**
4. Do you gamble more than once a month?
   yes   **no**
5. Do you make a considerable amount of spontaneous decisions each week?
   yes   **no**
6. Do you often feel empty after making those spontaneous decisions?
   yes   **no**
7. Are your casual conversations mostly about men, money, and/or materials things?
   yes   **no**
8. Do you watch a considerable amount of TV?
   yes   **no**
9. Do you lack a sense of accomplishment and purpose in your life?
   yes   **no**
10. Have you slept with more than one man in the last year, or are you involved with the wrong man and know it?
    yes   **no**

If you answered yes to at least three (3) of these questions you are probably spiritually bankrupt and in need of spiritual growth and awareness.

LIVING IN THE SPIRIT:
10 STEPS TO PRACTICE DAILY

1. Meditation - Meditate in the morning and at night. This is a great way to begin and end the day in the Spirit.

2. Daily Affirmations - Read a Bible verse and/or other spiritual affirmations throughout the day. This will keep you in a positive frame of mind and reaffirm the goals, dreams and desires that you want to achieve.

3. Think Before You Speak - Always practice this step. It will keep you from making negative statements or remarks and will also keep you from offending others with your language and gestures.

4. Exercise - Exercise in any form i.e., walking, jogging, aerobics, gardening, will keep your body in tune with your mind and spirit.

5. Hobbies - When you do something that you love and it involves creativity or giving back it brings harmony to your spirit and to the universe.

6. Read - Reading can also be a hobby, and it's the only way to feed your brain. Reading stimulates the brain and allows the mind to think, therefore, you learn. Try to learn something everyday.

7. OPP - Other People's Problems - restrain from getting emotionally, financially and spiritually involved in other people's problems and issues. This does not mean turn your back or not help or show support. It means being unattached and drawing the line when other's use their problems and issues to throw you off track of your own dreams and ambitions.

8. Love - Say, "I love you," to your loved ones as you greet each other on the phone or in person. Also, say, "I love you," to yourself and give yourself a hug.

9. Smile - Smile, because God loves you. Remember to smile, even when things are going wrong. A smile keeps the tension and stress from building in your face and head. A simple smile tells your spirit that everything is going to work out fine.

10. Be Thankful - Need I say more. Always be thankful to God, to everyone and to everything that happens in your life. Giving thanks for the good and the bad allows your spirit to always be at peace.

LIVING ON PURPOSE

Prayer - is the main key to living a purposeful life. Always pray.

Plan - have a plan for your purpose and work your plan daily.

Persevere - means to continue to strive for your goals no matter what obstacles get in the way.

Preparation- remember that success happens when preparation and opportunity meet. Prepare for success by working your plan daily.

Practice - always practice what you teach, preach, sing, write, or speak. This will ensure that you live a life of truth.

Patience - is a virtue that comes with faith. Remember that God is an on time God, so don't be too anxious.

Positive - always keep a positive attitude and stay surrounded by positive people.

Praise - always give God the praise for your accomplishments and success.

Power - exercise your creative power in everything you do. Also, remember you have the power in your life.

Prosperity - is the outcome for living your purpose. When you pray, plan, persevere, prepare, practice, be patient, stay positive, give praise, and exercise your power, you're on purpose, therefore, you live a prosperous life.

These are the P's for living a life with purpose.

Anfra Boyd

THE VOW OF CELIBACY

I take the vow of celibacy:

To abstain from sex

To purge my body of all unclean acts, thoughts and behavior

To honor my body as a temple of God

To wait until God unites me in marriage with my spiritual mate

To respect myself and learn self-love and self-worth

To listen to my inner spirit, and return to my spiritual path

To bring peace to my mind, body, and spirit

To protect myself from AIDS and other STD's

To tap into my creative power and inner strength

To give birth to my purpose in life

Sisters, let's stop dying of AIDS and start living for God.

COPING WITH LONELINESS

Loneliness is an emotion that affects more than 80% of women. It's not just the idea or thought of being alone or without a significant other; it's the fact that this loneliness is often fueled by an emptiness, an unfulfilled purpose and a lack of meaning in our lives. We try to disguise this emptiness with designer clothes, flashy boyfriends, and high-powered careers, but inside we know that something is missing. We crave something more, but don't know what it is. That something more is our purpose in life.

When we don't have a purpose, we make lonely choices and lonely decisions when it comes to relationships. As a result of those lonely choices and decisions our lives become littered with many failed relationships, abusive liaisons, and unrequited love(less) affairs. But there is a solution for single women.

Keeping busy, being creative and giving back to the community are practical and wholesome ways to cope with loneliness. Fill your life with the love of the universe and the loneliness will eventually go away. Remember, being alone does not mean that you have to be lonely.

Here are a few suggestions:

1. Continue your education
2. Get involved in church
3. Teach a class in your field of expertise
4. Learn a second language
5. Mentor a child
6. Volunteer at an AIDS hospice or nursing home
7. Become a community activist on (drug abuse, child abuse, battered women, drunk drivers)
8. Take a class on self-defense, dancing, yoga, etc.
9. Learn to play a musical instrument
10. Read books or write a book (we all have a story to tell)
11. Start or join a book club
12. Start your own business – open a book store, travel agency, arts & crafts shop, or eatery
13. Get into nature – plant a garden, learn horticulture
14. Start a walking club in your neighborhood
15. Learn a new sport – tennis, swimming, bowling, volleyball, or golf

THE WOMAN IN THE MIRROR
SELF-INVENTORY CHECK LIST

AM I?	YES	NO	SOME-TIMES	NEEDS IMPV
A good listener	☐	☐	☐	☐
A positive thinker	☐	☐	☐	☐
Understanding	☐	☐	☐	☐
Forgiving	☐	☐	☐	☐
A negative thinker	☐	☐	☐	☐
An independent thinker	☐	☐	☐	☐
A complainer	☐	☐	☐	☐
Encouraging	☐	☐	☐	☐
Inspiring	☐	☐	☐	☐
Open-minded	☐	☐	☐	☐
Selfish	☐	☐	☐	☐
A procrastinator	☐	☐	☐	☐
A liar	☐	☐	☐	☐
Demanding	☐	☐	☐	☐
Argumentative	☐	☐	☐	☐
Controlling	☐	☐	☐	☐
Ambitious	☐	☐	☐	☐
Envious	☐	☐	☐	☐
Self-centered	☐	☐	☐	☐
Materialistic	☐	☐	☐	☐
A perfectionist	☐	☐	☐	☐

THE WOMAN IN THE MIRROR
SELF-INVENTORY CHECK LIST

AM I?	YES	NO	SOME-TIMES	NEEDS IMPV
Hostile	☐	☐	☐	☐
Arrogant	☐	☐	☐	☐
Giving	☐	☐	☐	☐
A role model	☐	☐	☐	☐
A cheater	☐	☐	☐	☐
Spiritual	☐	☐	☐	☐
Religious	☐	☐	☐	☐
Giving back to my community	☐	☐	☐	☐
Happy with my life	☐	☐	☐	☐
Doing my life's work	☐	☐	☐	☐
Involved with the wrong man	☐	☐	☐	☐

THE WOMAN IN THE MIRROR
SELF-INVENTORY CHECK LIST

DO I?	YES	NO	SOME-TIMES	NEEDS IMPV
Share my resources with others	☐	☐	☐	☐
Hoard my money	☐	☐	☐	☐
Spend money foolishly	☐	☐	☐	☐
Invest my finances	☐	☐	☐	☐
Consider myself a true friend	☐	☐	☐	☐
Respect myself	☐	☐	☐	☐
Respect my sisters	☐	☐	☐	☐
Look down on others	☐	☐	☐	☐
Have to have a man in my life	☐	☐	☐	☐
Practice safe sex	☐	☐	☐	☐
Know my HIV status	☐	☐	☐	☐
Have sex on the first date	☐	☐	☐	☐
Spend quiet time alone	☐	☐	☐	☐
Date married men	☐	☐	☐	☐
Know my purpose in life	☐	☐	☐	☐
Offend others when I speak	☐	☐	☐	☐
Criticize others	☐	☐	☐	☐
Give of my time to help others	☐	☐	☐	☐
Practice celibacy	☐	☐	☐	☐
Think before I speak	☐	☐	☐	☐
Have a bad temper	☐	☐	☐	☐
Work better under pressure	☐	☐	☐	☐
Live my life on the edge	☐	☐	☐	☐
Like being the center of attention	☐	☐	☐	☐

Anfra Boyd

A NEW AGENDA

(List 10 major areas of your life that you want to change and why?)

1. _____

2. _____

3. _____

4. _____

5. _____

6. _____

7. _____

8. _____

9. _____

10. _____

VISION STATEMENT

This is your vision statement. Write down the things that you want to accomplish by the 21st Century and your plan of action. Also include the changes you need to make in order to reach your goals and improve your quality of life.

_____

_____

_____

_____

_____

_____

_____

_____

_____

_____

_____

_____

VISION STATEMENT

_____

_____

_____

_____

_____

_____

_____

_____

_____

_____

_____

_____

SPIRITUAL MATE
(FOR SINGLE WOMEN ONLY)

Write down ten important qualities that you want your spiritual mate to possess.

1. _____

2. _____

3. _____

4. _____

5. _____

6. _____

7. _____

8. _____

9. _____

10. _____

SPIRITUAL MATE
(FOR SINGLE WOMEN ONLY)

Write down ten important qualities that you have to share with your spiritual mate.

1. _____

2. _____

3. _____

4. _____

5. _____

6. _____

7. _____

8. _____

9. _____

10. _____

SINGLE WOMEN IN RELATIONSHIPS

Am I secure in the relationship?

yes   no   sometimes   not at all

Is he secure in the relationship?

yes   no   sometimes   not at all

Is he **married** or **single**? (Circle one)

Do I have a pattern of dating the wrong men?

yes   no   sometimes   not at all

Am I obsessive in the relationship?

yes   no   sometimes   not at all

Is he obsessive in the relationship?

yes   no   sometimes   not at all

Am I possessive in the relationship?

yes   no   sometimes   not at all

Is he possessive in the relationship?

yes   no   sometimes   not at all

Is he physically, mentally or verbally abusive?

yes   no   sometimes   not at all

Are we growing together spiritually?

yes   no   sometimes   not at all

Am I lonely in the relationship?

yes   no   sometimes   not at all

Do I want to marry him?

yes   no   sometimes   not at all

Does he want to marry me?

yes   no   sometimes   not at all

Is he romantic?

yes   no   sometimes   not at all

Anfra Boyd

SINGLE WOMEN IN RELATIONSHIPS

Is he affectionate?

    yes   no   **sometimes**   **not at all**

Is he considerate?

    yes   no   **sometimes**   **not at all**

Do we practice safe sex?

    yes   no   **sometimes**   **not at all**

Is he a loser?

    yes   no   **sometimes**   **not at all**

Does he love me?

    yes   no   **sometimes**   **not at all**

Does he respect me?

    yes   no   **sometimes**   **not at all**

Is he controlling?

    yes   no   **sometimes**   **not at all**

Is he responsible?

    yes   no   **sometimes**   **not at all**

Has he cheated on me?

    yes   no   **sometimes**   **not at all**

DO I LOVE HARD?

    yes   no   **sometimes**   **not at all**

Does he financially support me?

    yes   no   **sometimes**   **not at all**

Is he using me in any way?

    yes   no   **sometimes**   **not at all**

Am I afraid of being alone?

    yes   no   **sometimes**   **not at all**

Is he mentally stable?

    yes   no   **sometimes**   **not at all**

MY BETTER HALF

(*FOR MARRIED WOMEN ONLY*)

Does my husband satisfy me completely?

    yes   **no**   **sometimes**   **not at all**

Do I satisfy him completely?

    yes   **no**   **sometimes**   **not at all**

Has he ever cheated?

    yes   **no**   **sometimes**   **not at all**

Have I cheated on him?

    yes   **no**   **sometimes**   **not at all**

Is he my soul-mate?

    yes   **no**   **sometimes**   **not at all**

Are we growing together spiritually?

    yes   **no**   **sometimes**   **not at all**

Do I still love him?

    yes   **no**   **sometimes**   **not at all**

Am I in love with him?

    yes   **no**   **sometimes**   **not at all**

Am I lonely in the relationship?

    yes   **no**   **sometimes**   **not at all**

Did I marry him for the wrong reasons?

    yes   **no**   **sometimes**   **not at all**

Is he controlling?

    yes   **no**   **sometimes**   **not at all**

Is he demanding?

    yes   **no**   **sometimes**   **not at all**

Is he responsible?

    yes   **no**   **sometimes**   **not at all**

MY BETTER HALF

(*FOR MARRIED WOMEN ONLY*)

Does he support my dreams and ambitions?

yes   **no**   **sometimes**   **not at all**

Do I support his dreams and ambitions?

yes   **no**   **sometimes**   **not at all**

Am I glad I married him?

yes   **no**   **sometimes**   **not at all**

Can I make it without him financially?

yes   **no**   **sometimes**   **not at all**

Does he love me?

yes   **no**   **sometimes**   **not at all**

Do I want a divorce?

yes   **no**   **sometimes**   **not at all**

I am afraid of him?

yes   **no**   **sometimes**   **not at all**

Does he threaten me?

yes   **no**   **sometimes**   **not at all**

Do I want to spend the rest of my life with him?

yes   **no**   **sometimes**   **not at all**

Is he abusive physically, mentally or verbally?

yes   **no**   **sometimes**   **not at all**

If I could change one thing about him what would it be and why?

_____

_____

MARRIED MAN BLUES
(FOR WOMEN DATING MARRIED MEN)

Do I feel good about the relationship?

yes   no   sometimes   not at all

Do I want to be his wife someday?

yes   no   sometimes   not at all

Do I feel like I'm hurting his wife and family?

yes   no   sometimes   not at all

Do I feel cheated in the relationship?

yes   no   sometimes   not at all

Do I feel I'll pay for this mistake someday?

yes   no   sometimes   not at all

Does my conscious bother me?

yes   no   sometimes   not at all

Can I break up with him at anytime?

yes   no   sometimes   not at all

Is the relationship out in the open?

yes   no   sometimes   not at all

Does my family or children know about him?

yes   no   sometimes   not at all

Do I really love him?

yes   no   sometimes   not at all

Why Am I dating him?

_____

_____

_____

HOW TO TELL IF YOUR MAN IS THE WRONG MAN

	Yes	No
Is he married and not to you?	☐	☐
Is he living with you, in your home or apt?	☐	☐
Does he sell drugs?	☐	☐
Does he use drugs, i.e., marijuana, crack, etc.?	☐	☐
Does he drink more than socially?	☐	☐
Has he ever taken money or stolen from you?	☐	☐
Has he ever lied to you?	☐	☐
Does he not own a car and drives yours?	☐	☐
Do you pay any of his bills?	☐	☐
Does he change or quit his jobs often?	☐	☐
Has he ever cheated on you?	☐	☐
Does he make promises that he doesn't keep?	☐	☐
Does he have children that he doesn't support?	☐	☐
Does he disrespect his mother?	☐	☐
Does he live with his parents or another woman?	☐	☐
Is he irresponsible?	☐	☐
Does he have bad credit?	☐	☐

HOW TO TELL IF YOUR MAN IS THE WRONG MAN

	Yes	No
Does he lack ambition?	☐	☐
Does he not help around the house?	☐	☐
Does he not know how to change a flat tire?	☐	☐
Are you supporting him in any way?	☐	☐
Is he a liar?	☐	☐
Is he jealous?	☐	☐
Is he abusive?	☐	☐
Is he bisexual?	☐	☐
Has he ever been to jail for a felony?	☐	☐
Is he an excessive gambler?	☐	☐
Does he not believe in God?	☐	☐
Has he given you a sexually transmitted disease?	☐	☐

If you answered yes to at least one (1) of these questions, you are dating, married to, or involved with the wrong man!!

THE MEN IN MY LIFE

Write down all the men that you've been involved with sexually and why. Use this list to evaluate your dating practices and determine what your reasons for dating are and if you have a pattern of dating the wrong men. Also use this list to see if you've been exposed to the HIV virus. Add more pages if you need to, be honest with yourself and decide to make a change.

	NAME	YR	WHY
1.			
2.			
3.			
4.			
5.			
6.			
7.			
8.			
9.			
10.			

You Are My Sister

	NAME	**YR**	**WHY**
11.			
12.			
13.			
14.			
15.			
16.			
17.			
18.			
19.			
20.			

Anfra Boyd

	NAME	**YR**	**WHY**
21.			
22.			
23.			
24.			
25.			
26.			
27.			
28.			
29.			
30.			

You Are My Sister

	NAME	YR	WHY
31.			
32.			
33.			
34.			
35.			
36.			
37.			
38.			
39.			
40.			

	NAME	**YR**	**WHY**
41.			
42.			
43.			
44.			
45.			
46.			
47.			
48.			
49.			
50.			

You Are My Sister

LEGACY OF LIFE

What if today was your last day on earth, what would you leave behind as the legacy of your life? Write down the things that you've accomplished up to this day and what you would want the world to remember you by.

BOOK AVAILABLE THROUGH
F.I.G. PUBLISHING

YOU ARE MY SISTER
$12.95

TO ORDER YOUR AUTOGRAPHED COPY
MAIL CHECK OR MONEY ORDER
PAYABLE TO:

ANFRA BOYD
2760 CRACKLEROSE
MEMPHIS TN 38127

Name _____

Date _____

Address _____

City _____

State _____ Zip _____

# of books ordered _____ Total _____

Names books autographed to:

_____

** Books are $12.95 each, which includes taxes and shipping and handling if ordered my mail or Internet at: www.anfra.com